# THE
# PERFECT
# VEHICLE

# THE
# PERFECT
# VEHICLE

*What It Is About Motorcycles*

Melissa Holbrook Pierson

VIVE LE MOTOCYCLISME

W. W. NORTON & COMPANY
NEW YORK LONDON

6/97

Portions of this book previously appeared in *Harper's* and *The Threepenny Review*.

For information about permission to reproduce selections from this book, write to Permissions, W. W. Norton & Company, Inc., 500 Fifth Avenue, New York, New York 10110

The text of this book is composed in Janson
with the display set in Square 721
Composition by White River Publishing Services, W. Hartford, VT
Manufacturing by Quebecor Printing, Fairfield Inc.
Book Design by Chris Welch

Library of Congress Cataloging-in-Publication Data
Pierson, Melissa Holbrook.
      The perfect vehicle : what it is about motorcycles / Melissa
  Holbrook Pierson.
          p.      cm.
      **ISBN  0-393-04064-X**
      1. Motorcycling.  2. Motorcycles.  I. Title.
  GV1059.5.P54   1997
  796.75—DC20                                            96-35582
                                                            CIP

W. W. Norton & Company, Inc., 500 Fifth Avenue, New York, N.Y. 10110
                http://www.wwnorton.com

W. W. Norton & Company Ltd., 10 Coptic Street, London WC1A 1PU

1 2 3 4 5 6 7 8 9 0

For Luc Sante

*All things considered there are only two kinds of men in the world: those
that stay at home and those that do not.*
*—Rudyard Kipling*

*There are only two kinds of bikers: those that have been down and those
that are going to go down.*
*—Biker saying*

At precisely this moment someone, somewhere, is getting
ready to ride. The motorcycle stands in the cool, dark
garage, its air expectant with gas and grease. The rider
approaches from outside; the door opens with a whir and a bang. The
light goes on. A flame, everlasting, seems to rise on a piece of chrome.

As the rider advances, leather sleeves are zipped down tight on the
forearms, and the helmet briefly obliterates everything as it is pulled
on, the chin strap buckled. This muffled weight with its own faint
but permanent scent triggers recollection of the hours and days spent
within it. Soft leather gloves with studded palms, insurance against
the reflex of a falling body to put its hands out in midair, go on last.

The key is slipped into the ignition at the top of the steering head.
Then the rider swings a leg over the seat and sits but keeps the
weight on the balls of the feet. With a push from the thighs the rider
rocks the bike forward once, again, picking up momentum until it
starts to fall forward and down from the centerstand. At this moment
the rider pulls a lever with the first finger of the right hand, and the

brake pads close like a vise on the front wheel's iron rotor. At the almost instantaneous release of the brake, the bike rises slightly from the forks, which had telescoped under the heft. Now the 450 pounds of metal, fluid, and plastic rests in tenuous balance between the rider's legs; if it started to lean too much to one side, the weight that had lain low in a state of grace would suddenly assert itself in a manic bid to meet the concrete with a crash. Inherently unstable at a stand-still, the bike is waiting for the human to help it become its true self. Out there running, it can seem as solid as stone.

The key turns; the idiot lights glow. The green is for neutral gear, the red for the battery, another red for oil pressure. The starter but-ton on the right handlebar, pressed, begins a whirring below. A simul-taneous twist of the right grip pulls the throttle cables and the engine bleats, then gulps, then roars. There is contained fire within inches of the rider's knees. As the plugs in the two cylinders, posed in a 90-degree V, take their inestimably quick turns in sparking a volatile cocktail of fuel and compressed oxygen, the expanding gases forcing back the pistons, the machine vibrates subtly from side to side.

A flip of the headlight switch on the handlebar throws the garage walls to either side into theatrical relief. (The rider knows to run through all the lights—turn signals, taillight, brake lights tripped by hand and foot—to make sure they work, but is sometimes guilty of neglecting this step.) The rider pulls in the left-hand lever, then presses down with the left foot. There's a solid *chunk* as first gear engages.

In the neat dance that accomplishes many operations on a motor-cycle—one movement to countered by another fro, an equilibrium of give and take—the squeezed clutch lever is slowly let out while the other hand turns the throttle grip down. The bike moves out into a brighter world where the sun startles the rider's eyes for a moment and washes everything in a continual pour.

Out in the early-morning street there is little traffic, for which the rider sends up thanks: on a bike, cars are irksome, their slow-motion ways infuriating. Pulling out of the drive, the rider shifts into second, this time with the boot toe under the lever to push it up. The small jolt of increased speed from the rear wheel is experienced in the seat, just as in the elastic pause when a horse gathers strength in its haunches before springing into a canter from a trot.

To warm up the tires, the rider shifts so slightly in the seat it is hardly noticeable except to the bike, which dips left. Then quickly right again, then left, then right, until the machine is drawing a sinuous S down the road. They could dance like this all day, partnered closely and each anticipating the next step so surely it is not at all clear who is who.

As they reach the exurban limits and turn onto a narrow road that ascends among trees and infrequent stone houses set back in the shadows, other riders are accelerating up highway ramps; riding gingerly in first gear between two lanes of traffic jammed on a city bridge; hitting the dirt front-wheel-first after being launched from the top of a hillock in a field; trying to pass a motor home making its all-too-gradual way into a national park; feeling a charge move from stomach to chest as the bike straightens up from the deepest lean it's yet entered; following three friends also on bikes into the parking lot of a diner for coffee; slowing down, cursing, to the shoulder because the clutch cable broke.

Today, on the way to a particular, longed-for destination, while joy taken in the wheels' consuming revolutions conflates with the desire to arrive, the journey becomes one of combined anticipation of its end and pleasure in its duration. Riding is an occupation defined by duplicities.

Take the numbers: seven million who ride stacked against 225 million who don't. (To get an idea of the minority status this number confirms, consider the fact that some twenty million Americans call themselves dedicated birdwatchers.) Those who ride are both alone and held tight in the fold of the elect. They draw together for protective warmth and take strange relish in needing to do so at all. The glue between these relative few can be tenacious: a rider traveling through a small town, spotted by a rider who lives there, is—because of this simple fact—invited home and given food and advice. A rider stopped by the roadside, even for a cigarette, prompts another biker to stop and ask if help is needed. At the very least, barring the occasional internecine feud that can make motorcyclists embody a sort of nationalism on wheels, they wave as they pass one another. It's as if they all came from the same small burg where street greetings are as obligatory as wearing clothes.

The road, constantly turning, constantly offers up the possibility of something unexpected around the bend—gravel in a tumult across the road, a car drifting over the yellow line, a dog maddened by the din from the pipes. The rider processes data from the road and its environs with a certain detachment, translating them nearly as quickly into physical response: eat or be eaten. There is no room in the brain for idle thought (except on the highway, when idle thoughts appear and float and reconfigure in endless array), and a biker can go for miles and miles without waking up to any sudden realization, including the one that nothing at all has been thought for miles and miles. The faster you ride, the more closed the circuit becomes, deleting everything but this second and the next, which are hurriedly merging. Having no past to regret and no future to await, the rider feels free. Looked at from this tight world, the other one with its gore and stickiness seems well polished and contained at last.

This peculiar physiological effect, common to all high-concentration pursuits, may be why one finds among motorcyclists a large number of people who always feel as if there were a fire lit under them when they are sitting still. When they're out riding, the wind disperses the flame so they don't feel the terrible heat. The duration of the ride starts to be the only time they know happiness, so they go on longer and longer or for more and more rides, while their families become more and more unhappy. For a few, those who become racers, relief is to be had only at 160 mph down a straightaway. They simultaneously embrace and deny the risk, the worst outcome of which is confined to accidents, that which is outside the norm. But the norm stands for much less here than it does elsewhere, and the realm of accident is much larger. Instead of admitting to insanity to want to live in such a place, they imagine their way out of it: Well, if I fall, I'll land on the tires or hay bales or grass berm. Then I'll pick up the bike and if it's not too badly damaged I'll finish the race. That's what they're prepared to allow. Their once colorful leathers are scuffed gray and held together with duct tape.

Every rider of a motorcycle lives with a little of the same denial, which is after all healthy and spares us from living in a world made entirely of dread. It is also the price of admission to a day like this. If the rider wants, the throttle can be cracked open so suddenly the handlebars yank the arms, threatening to run away with that paltry creature on back now reduced to hanging on and enjoying the ride.

The roar left to ring under the trees as the machine passes is like the laser arc of red drawn by a taillight in a long-exposure photograph at night. It is the ghost remnant of how the bike cleaved the air, and what the rider felt as gravity battled flight against the rider's body. The curves play games with the rider, and the rider is lost in the concentration it takes to match wits with an impressive opponent. How fast to enter this turn? The fact that you can be sadly mistaken is what gives the right choice its sweet taste.

But the rider has never known a fear quite like the one when riding just ahead is the object of deep affection. Flying along in tandem, an invisible wire stretched between them to connect the distance through a moving world, the one looks to the other like an insect clinging to the frenzied body of its prey. The rider, behind, watches this transformed human and sees right through the leathers to the tender skin as it looked while sleep was upon it. In one flash the rider sees how laughably easy it would be for something to happen. It is that pernicious distance between them that does the trick: a few yards that is an unbridgeable gap. Perhaps it's all projection—that the rider, looking toward the other, at once feels how vulnerable the self truly is. But isn't that what love is anyway? In hoping for the other, you realize how much you hope for yourself?

When things conspire—the traffic is thick and wild, the sun is leaving moment by moment, rain slicks the surface of the road—the rider best understands what can otherwise remain hidden: that a motorcyclist is both the happy passenger on an amusement park ride and its earnest operator. The rider splits into two, navigating between vacation and dire responsibility.

As the road leaves home farther and farther behind, it makes its own friendly advances to keep the rider happy: See, this is where you stopped your bike once and ate an apple from the tank bag and took off your boots to feel the damp grass beneath your socks; this is the place your beloved bought you a handful of fireballs when you stopped for gas. And there is always the chance that the unexpected around the bend may turn out not to be a danger to avoid, but a sight or smell that appears suddenly like a check in the mail.

Now, with a hundred miles on the clock, the going has taken on a life of its own. The rider has nearly forgotten what it means to sit anywhere but on this seat; the eyes are swinging back and forth in unchanging rhythm like sonar. Brake; slow; lean; heat up. Brake; slow; lean; heat up. Again and again until it's a rocking chair, a hundred freestyle laps, a hand absently stroking the skin.

The road's painted line, a vanishing point in reverse, is eaten up under the wheels, like a video game where the landscape flashes past while the vehicle stays put. The wind is a steady reassurance on the chest. The rider now becomes susceptible to white-line fever, which feels not so much like a need to continue on forever but as if all options for anything else have been removed. It is simple: the power to go, the power to stop, are as reduced as a metaphor and made to fit in one small hand. The rider, naturally, fears this state. And, keen on the perversity that always hides deep in pleasure, the rider, who is me, wants nothing more.

# THE
# PERFECT
# VEHICLE

*A machine is like a desert. Either it fascinates or appalls you.*
—*Wilfrid Noyce*, The Springs of Adventure

From my mother I learned to write prompt thank-you notes for a variety of occasions; from Mrs. King's ballroom dancing school I learned a proper curtsy and, believe it or not, what to do if presented with nine eating utensils at the same place setting, presumably at the home of the hosts to whom I had just curtsied. From motorcycles I learned practically everything else.

In the ten years that I've been on and around them, motorcycles have given me plenty of metaphoric chalk talks. There has been a lot about the nature of the arbitrary, the grace of sudden change. The illustrations are curious. One day, say, you can be in graduate school, sweating over blazingly irrelevant papers on *Sir Gawain and the Green Knight* and yet another reading of Hawthorne, looking forward to a life behind library stacks and lecterns while wearing muted silk scarves and subtle glasses. And the next you can be out of there so entirely you have grease beneath your fingernails as you bump-start your bike down a hill after a fuse blew, or you wake up extra early on

Sunday morning to make the seventy miles to the parking lot of a diner in Danbury, Connecticut, just to gaze upon the sight of a couple hundred bikes that are there because of the same impulse. Or perhaps none of this is so strange after all and I am merely fulfilling the appraisal of William F. Buckley, Jr., who called all of us in my college class "ferocious illiterates" after we disinvited him from giving our graduation address in 1980.

A motorcycle becomes an extension of yourself, your body and faculties and hopes and pathologies—and I learned that mine could give me the sort of information it is painful to receive, which is how you know (according to psychologists) it is true. In holding out the need to maintain and repair it, my motorcycle would quickly transform itself into a mirror at the moment I raised the wrench toward it, so that I was really turning bolts inside myself, the ones that confusingly wished to come cleanly out and at the same time were stuck fast, apparently waiting for someone better than me to rescue them from myself. I also appreciated the teachings of the other bolts, such as the ones holding the brake rotors to the front wheel, which wouldn't budge no matter how hard I whaled on them or with what, just as I was especially grateful for the ones under the valve covers that I learned to adjust perfectly, taking small increments and making them smaller in order to reach the point of equilibrium when the feeler gauge under the tappets is held just snugly enough, a point attained by sensation and nothing else. That is true satisfaction.

There were some interesting global lessons, too, like the simple but easily overlooked fact that alone of animals we are primarily marked by our passions. For some it's the Grateful Dead; for others Gilbert and Sullivan. Partisans of old Airstreams follow other Airstream lovers across the country to meet at rallies and celebrate the object of their affection as well as the fact that they found one another. Then there is the inexplicable obsession shared only by train spotters, for whom no explanation is needed. Some Americans seem to have no hobby at all, you say? Certainly they do, if the definition of a hobby is something that takes up all your time, love, and extra cash: that would be children. And then there are motorcycles, which are just like children to some of their owners, the hard core.

I am not referring to outlaw bikers. A small minority of all riders, the highly visible, self-proclaimed one-percenters (as they consider their numbers in relation to those of the less colorful majority), have perhaps understandably taken the spotlight. Still, if I see yet another glossy photo essay on tattooed hellions accompanied by earnest text explaining to a horrified but titillated Middle America that their bikes are called "hogs," I think I'll scream.

Of course, there are "gangs" (they call themselves clubs, as do most clubs that are in no way gangs). If you're wearing the patch, or colors, of your club on the back of your jacket as you ride through the territory claimed by, say, the Pagans, they will request that you furl your flag. The Hell's Angels still exist, too, although they remain a very small fraction of all motorcyclists and have perhaps graduated from the quaint type of brutal mischief catalogued in Hunter S. Thompson's 1966 *Hell's Angels*. They are today, according to a news item quoting international police intelligence sources, a "world crime threat" and "as likely to drive a BMW series 7 as a motorcycle." As for the public fixation on these lively few, I am finding it increasingly tedious, as if the night only consisted of one moonrise and not a billion stars too. It is perhaps understandable, given our desire to see humans as capable of anything; either extreme of behavior or achievement will apparently do the trick. If we actually looked at the vast interior cordoned off by these two points, however, we would find ourselves. Anything as unexamined as the normal heart has got to have a few interesting things to be said about it.

Another of those aha lessons concerned group allegiance, that which leads warriors to die behind the banner of their nation. It is present in even the smallest domains, as any partisan of competitive sports well knows. In order to determine one's group affiliation, however, one has to define the group. People with brown skin and straight hair? People who believe that if they strap on a suicide bomb and enter a public square filled with heathens they will become heroes in heaven? Thus among some bikers there is an argument going on that ranges from barely voiced to openly acrimonious: What is a "real" biker? Contrary to expectation, it does not date to the recent fashionableness of motorcycles (primarily Harleys) among people who in previous decades might have incredulously denied the possibility that they would ever look twice at a motorcycle, much less with longing. These people are called RUBs (rich urban bikers), in part because these days one must have a zippy acronym for everything. Long before the age of the RUBs, however, bikers were delimiting themselves. A few have always refused to get entangled, professing a noble egalitarianism: anyone who likes bikes is a biker. But the main grist of letters columns in bike magazines the world over is the exchange of accusations that one type or another of biker, being untrue, is ruining the reputation of the sport. A French book from 1973 called *Toute La Moto* describes how the sides take sides:

> Bikers can be grouped into two classes: true bikers and sham bikers. The identikit of a true biker as seen by the other kind is of a roughneck, helmeted and booted, unshaven and with hands blackened with axle grease. He can additionally be wet and muddy. The picture is complete if his bike is falling apart, held together with bits of wire, constantly breaking down but paradoxically continuing to run, and with a chain which, thank God, constantly needs adjusting, since the chain is the best means for dirtying one's hands.
>
> The true biker rides four hundred kilometers in the rain to attend a rally, rides winter and summer, walks bowlegged from riding, talks about his cornering and his falls, and, when entering a bar, slams open the door and announces his presence by yelling.
>
> And here's how the true biker views his opposite number: wears a suit, rides rarely and then only on the Champs-Elysées. His bike is all shiny chrome. He needs to have chicks eyeing him. His han-

dlebars are huge. His bike is a phallic symbol because he is laden with complexes.

Except for the yelling in bars, almost every motorcyclist I've encountered combines elements from both types. (The French are, anyway, perhaps too sensitive to appearances and show it with the attention to detail that prompts magazines like *Actuel* to publish extensive typologies contrasting *les bikers*, Harley aficionados, and *les sportifs*, Japanese superbike riders, by cataloguing the favored costume, books, idols, and hangouts of each.) My own answer to the question would have to comprise all who have heard a bike sing and thought it one of the most stirring melodies they've ever heard; who have wished that in this moment all the cars in the country would disappear to some junkyard far away; who know a perfect road is defined by its curves, camber, view; who look at bikes, and look for bikes, wherever they happen to be.

The hardcore lover of motorcycles, the one whose head turns at every growing sound that promises a bike will soon flash into view, can't help it. There is a peculiar kind of motolust that inspires some people to fill their garages with bikes and the "pre-restored" carcasses thereof and still be unable to resist the next one they see that has a for-sale sign around its neck. They go away for a weekend of riding and come back with new friends whom they stay up with half the night talking of bikes and other destinations at which they will meet new people who will phone them the following week to tell of further destinations. The calendar fills; the season is not long enough. The pocketbook is rarely large enough, for bikes, like boats, are black holes in the universe of money.

Riding on a motorcycle can make you feel joyous, powerful, peaceful, frightened, vulnerable, and back out to happy again, perhaps in the same ten miles. It is life compressed, its own answer to the question "Why?"

Why? they ask, those who don't ride. Those who do ride are incapable of understanding the question. Riding feels good, they say—it feels damn good. But I think there is more, just as there is always more underneath the obvious, and a little more underneath that. The great layered mysteries of human motivation are oddly both variegated and amazingly uniform. And they are revealed in the many reasons, as well as the one simple one, why people ride.

Motorcycles are what they feel like (profoundly sensual—vroom, vroom—and perhaps a bit primordial) and also what they look like (fearsome, with a strange deep beauty). Look at that engine, out for anyone to see, and those two simple wheels: what else announces its intent so brazenly? It is not simply a coincidence that after World War II some ill-fitting veterans came home to ride these particular machines in angry bunches, giving birth to the myth and reality of gangs like the Hell's Angels. Just as it was not insignificant that T. E. Lawrence bought the farm, riding back from the post office at a very reasonable rate of speed, on one of his beloved Brough Superiors.

Colin Wilson counted Lawrence among the exemplary "outsiders" in his book of the same name, and he explained the adventurer's central motive: "His clear-sighted intellect could not conceive of moral freedom without physical freedom too; pain was an invaluable instrument in experiments to determine the extent of his moral freedom." Motorcyclists intuitively understand this even if they cannot articulate it, just as they would identify with Lawrence's penchant for riding his lovely machine, which he named Boanerges, flat-out for speed, and sometimes to race a fighter plane flying overhead. "A skittish motor-bike with a touch of blood in it is better than all the riding animals on earth, because of its logical extension of our faculties, and the hint, the provocation, to excess conferred by its honeyed untired smoothness," he wrote. "Because Boa loves me, he gives me five more miles of speed than a stranger would get from him."

Motorcyclists understand this too, because what bikes feel like is an extension of the self—a better you, a perfectible, fixable you, an ominously powerful you. That is also what they look like to the occasionally cowed bystander, who, like an Indian first seeing a white man on horseback, may believe he has encountered some new creature that is only part human.

To those who love motorcycles deeply, there is usually one aspect of the machine that broadcasts its allure in advance of all others. It may be the visual arrangement of parts, their rake and line and organization that come together in a design that seems to freeze speed. It may be the look of meanness, sweetness, or promise delivered even from under the fluorescent light of the showroom. For me, it is their sound that makes the heart race. The exhaust note of certain bikes functions like an aria, the relentlessly plaintive song that arrives at the vulnerable moment in the opera to wring the emotions dry.

Every model has its characteristic melody, and maybe if you love your bike you simply love its sound most. (Harley-Davidson is now attempting to trademark the sound of its engine against pretenders who would seek to duplicate the tune of a 45-degree V-twin with a single crank pin.) The sounds of Italian engines, especially those of Moto Guzzis and Ducatis, are to me so supremely sensuous that I can only merely appreciate—albeit appreciate well—the tone of other bikes. And believe me, I am not alone: the Swedish Ducati Club has produced a CD titled *Ducati Passions*, a recording of a dozen different models of the renowned machines from Bologna, from a 1958 55/e to a 1993 M900 Monster, as they move up and down the gears; the liner notes include information on each bike's exhaust system and warn overenthusiastic listeners to take it easy with the volume so as not to blow their speakers.

My friend Erica, who when we were children loved horses with a passion that has only been equaled by what she now feels for bikes, owns a Moto Guzzi and a Ducati. She is known to swoon at the sound of their kin on the street or track, but she is not tone-deaf to the other great songs of the motorcycle world, either. As a vintage British BSA Gold Star went by, her eyes grew larger and larger and she exclaimed with childlike amazement, "It's like the heavens have opened up!" A British writer—the Brits are especially finely attuned to the poetry of the man-made world—described the sound of a Yamaha enduro model as "a shopful of timpani getting showered with marbles."

I would know the sound of a big Guzzi in my sleep. It concentrates its aural energies in your upper chest, ringing through your bones. It's not the fat blatting of a Harley—the heavy metal of exhaust music—often released at unbelievable levels by aftermarket pipes, nor is it the sheer scream of a high-revving Japanese crotch rocket. It is, rather, the sound of joy, as is, say, the bass tune of a Ducati 851 roaring inches away down the straightaway of a racetrack at well over 100 mph. The sight is a flash of red, impossible to see except as a blur at close range, but the swelling, deepening waves of sound as it retreats stay with you, pinning you solidly to the ground through your feet.

In the quite dignified old suburb of Akron, Ohio, where I grew up, the warm months were full of soft sibilance: crickets rasping, moths hitting screen, the *shk-shk* of sprinklers at dusk. On rare occasions, obviously lost on those streets lined with large Tudor homes harboring large station wagons and Lincoln Continentals in their Tudor garages, a motorcycle would rip the summer quiet. I would feel a sudden little annoyance in my small soul, already proprietary and judgmental; how odd, what an accidental gift, to grow up and one day walk through an unmarked door and find myself in the alternative universe of motorcycles and motorcyclists, where I would be shown, gently and with a patience I barely deserved, what a mistake I'd made.

I am a motorcyclist, and though I recognize I am not the "usual" motorcyclist, I also don't anticipate ever meeting one of those in person. All I know is that over the years I have occasionally sat back and thought how strange it is that motorcycles can completely overtake your being and act as if they own it. Certainly nothing in my life before them—and certainly not my parents, whose own interests run to chamber music, books, gardening, art, and cocktail parties—had prepared me to fall in love with bikes. I had gone through prep school, college, graduate school without knowing they existed. Those years were filled with sequential or concurrent passions: horses, the Civil War, dogs, bicycling, photography, poetry, the dream of true socialism, literary theory, and a couple dozen boys. I am still interested in all those things to some extent, except for the boyfriends, whose names I have largely forgotten, but the desire I came to feel for bikes eclipsed all of them, even though I still dream of having a horse.

Of all the things that could have happened to that girl when she grew up, motorcycles are fairly far down on the imaginable list. But now I can't imagine it otherwise. The whole thing reminds me of the story my father tells of when he was presented by his uncle with an awkwardly wrapped present; a metal point protruded from the top of the package. With a challenging swagger, Uncle Harold said, "Bet you can't guess what this is!"

Since it was utterly impossible to tell, my father figured he'd come up with the most absurd thing he could. "Why, it's a statue of Don Quixote, and that's his lance!" he proclaimed.

Uncle Harold's face fell. "How did you know?" he asked in suspicious deflation.

*This book is dedicated to all those men who betrayed me at one time or*
*another, in hopes they will fall off their motorcycles and break their necks.*
—*Diane Wakoski, dedication to* The Motorcycle Betrayal Poems

L et's call him Tad, and me ready. He was a sculptor, or maybe
a composer, and he rode motorcycles. His laugh was wicked,
and he had pursued me so hard my objections became
briefly pro forma before falling without a further complaint: he acted
certain that I was desirable, something of which I was not convinced
but wished to be. And so he looked desirable in turn to me, with his
equally abiding faith in the worth of his art and his ideas and his taste,
and the ease and joy with which he moved through the world. He was
a natural person, one who simply lived and who rarely got angry. He
was intent upon his craft and ambitious for its success. He liked good
food and played good music on good stereo equipment. When he got
a new kitten, he would say, "Watch this!" and launch her, twisting
through the air, toward the other side of his sizable loft. He maintained that she liked it, and it is possible that she did.

Here was his typical day: on site with the construction crew, home
to the loft for lunch, a phone call to me while lounging on the couch

next to the coal stove that was necessary in a place where you could see your breath in the winter but illegal in New York City, all afternoon and early evening in the studio mud-wrestling highflown ideas into submission with the help of a little Jack Daniel's, and then I would come over and we would get on a low, black Ducati 350 and scream over the Manhattan Bridge and debark in front of Bar Lui or El Internacional. There, some guy passing by would stop to stare or someone would get up from a sidewalk table and come over to ask questions about the little bike with the come-hither looks and voice to match. That a three-fifty? Nineteen sixty-eight? No kidding—a desmo? Is it hard to tune, et cetera, et cetera? Tad answered the questions about his rare old bike and I quietly dissolved into the sidewalk.

Such is the fate of a woman without a motorcycle in the company of a man who has one, not to mention three, all Italian, one of which has desmodromic valves. But nothing remains the same for long.

One afternoon Tad lay on the selfsame couch, reading an issue of *Cycle World,* the kind of boilerplate publication that with minor changes serves aficionados of audio equipment, cars, bowhunting, or homemade ceramics. He sat up and tossed it to me. There's an article on page forty-three that might interest you, and he went to make some coffee.

How innocent the gesture; yes, well, how innocent they always are. I read through the piece on taking a beginning rider's course taught by Motorcycle Safety Foundation instructors. In a matter of minutes I had dialed the 800 number that appeared in the article and was talking to someone who took my zip code and returned with the news that Trama's Auto School in Queens offered a course, which would be held over two successive summer weekends.

It was a little like watching a light bulb go on over someone's head, only the head is yours and the light bulb is an elaborate blinking neon arrangement that spells out *WHY DIDN'T YOU THINK OF THIS BEFORE?* My face must have exhibited the weird blend of wary surprise and pure happiness that one sees move over the features of so many women who first see another woman go by on a bike: Of *course*! It is now possible, because I have *seen* it.

In the perfect and concise phrase of a friend of mine, who ought to know, given that his garage is packed wall to wall with them, motorcycles are charismatic objects. People are rarely neutral on the subject, neither those for whom they act as a second heart, nor those who think them a tool of misfortune. The Greek word *charisma* means "favor, gift," and my dictionary adds an apt cross-reference: "see under *yearn*."

Even now, after so many accumulated days, weeks, months on their backs, so many miles, sights, memories that mix with others to give off the scent of dreamlike improbability, I rarely think of motorcycles without a little yearning. They are about moving, and humans, I think, yearn to move—it's in our cells, in our desires. We quiet our babies with cyclic movement, and we quiet ourselves by going.

Before that moment of revelation while holding a copy of *Cycle World*, I had the prerequisites without knowing it: a love of speed for its own sake, the need for constant movement, and the desire to be different, or at least to be seen that way—perhaps to be seen in the first place. And one doesn't ride motorcycles if one wishes to remain invisible.

So it begins. You learn the basics of how to ride, make mistakes, not too serious if you're lucky, learn some more, futz around. Buy a bike and learn to fix it, because the fixing and the accompanying flush of self-sufficiency are part of bikes' allure in an increasingly monolithic, unfixable world. Go on lots of rides, alone, with good friends and occasionally near strangers, and alone some more. Spend the week waiting for the weekend. Grow to love traveling so much you begin to feel that only by going places can you be at rest. Build a world made of maps and of dreams of using all of them. Maybe start to hate humankind for procreating with such stupid abandon, thereby daily stealing vistas and giving them to strip malls and condo villages, and taking snaky two-lanes through the trees and straightening them out under a hot sun and crapping them up with stores selling ever more repetitive products to the excrescence of consumers who sit idling in their cars and blocking the way for you to get out of there, out of there.

You become a member of a community, linked first and foremost to anyone who rides; when another bike passes, you take your left hand off the bar and give the Wave, and perhaps a thumbs-up if it's a particularly splendid day or road. Then you begin to notice the differences that mark all of you, because you are human and humans are animals for whom making distinctions is a primary drive like sex or hunger or, for New England farmers a century ago, building low stone walls. If none exist, you make up some even finer distinctions. Riders of Harley-Davidsons, at the moment the most popular bike in the world, have eyes largely for each other; an ad for the brand once pictured a biceps tattooed with the Harley eagle and rhetorically asked what other name commanded similar loyalty. Japanese sport-bike riders, perhaps too plentiful for real closeness, can be too preoc-cupied with the turns they're happily throwing themselves into or so new to this week's thrill sport they have not yet understood the true benefits and deficits of being a member of a 3 percent minority in the United States. The pilots of the interstates' great land yachts, Yamaha Ventures or Honda Gold Wings, hang with other "Wingnuts" on their way to the gatherings they call "Wingdings," although they are often friendly and talkative to riders of any other two-wheeler. (Gold Wings are referred to not too uncharitably as Lead Wings, due to their status as the Lincoln Continental of bikes: eight hundred pounds, six cylinders, 1500cc, 100 hp, electric reverse, an aviation-style Bank Angle Indicator, all dressed in gold and chrome accents, tufted Naugahyde seats with passenger armrests, and stereo tapedeck.)

With a few notable exceptions, aficionados of British machines like vintage Triumphs and Nortons rarely go far on their cantankerous mounts, but they'll nod appreciatively from their sidewalk fix-it sessions when another cool bike goes by. Some BMW owners, generally proud and sometimes downright crazy (something the Germans would no doubt take a dim view of), are so enthusiastically proud they have split from the other half of BMW riders, giving the United States two national organizations of Beemer confederates, those for whom biking is a way to get to the party and those for whom the party is biking—while wearing proper protective gear at all times. Their bikes having many of the same virtues, and their riders interested equally in good-looking gimcracks and the low-down beauty of pure utility, those with BMWs and those with Moto Guzzis rib each other good-naturedly about the reliability of the machines they like to put in five-hundred-mile days on. Frequently they are the same person.

On a motorcycle, sometimes the world seems small and sometimes it doesn't. I just finished a ride of more than four hundred miles without seeing another person on a motorcycle. People traveling alongside me in cars on I-80 across Pennsylvania stared; children would point, and young men would look as if they had just seen whatever was most impossible appear before their very eyes. If another biker had in fact passed me without returning my wave, as sometimes happens, it would have felt a lonely blow.

There have been times I've wanted to shout, as if I were frustrated on the other side of a wall of Plexiglas, *It's me! I'm still me*, though I'm wearing this black outfit and I rode here on something that's been known (I apologize) to set off particularly sensitive car alarms as we go by. But the simple fact of the costume puts me inside the ant farm, where I am watched. It's not just a matter of people who make assumptions or who discriminate, although I remember those best. I remember riding up to Storm King sculpture park near West Point one summer day and getting turned away by a guard who looked disdainful and disbelieving; a couple of years before I had been waved smilingly through when I arrived in a car with a picnic basket and some friends who looked as though they could have been a literature professor, a financier, and a ballet dancer, because they were. *I am still me!* I wanted to shout at the guard while shaking him smartly. I remember riding up to the college I had spent four years at; I knew that during the day one could simply drive through the academic-Gothic gate and up to Main building. But when I tried to do so, the sentry came awake and leaped out at me, yelling, "Hey! Stop! Where are you going?" Visiting, I said; he stood there. I am an alumna, I continued, and he looked perplexed for a minute, then told me motorcycles were not allowed on campus. I would have to park just inside the gate, next to the door I had entered three mornings a week for a year to watch slides of the world's great art click by in the dark. I remember, most angrily, being turned away late one chill evening in North Carolina from a bed-and-breakfast with only a couple of cars in its lot; we were miles from any other inn, and so tired I wanted to sit down on the neat lawn and cry. *I am still me!* I would have said. Or am I?

Ever since the door onto the world of motorcycles opened I have been trying to comprehend what it was we were doing, and why. People tell me I think too much, but I don't see how such a thing is possible, unless of course it is either in the middle of sex or at the apex of a high-speed turn. The subculture of bikes, as with any fellowship that develops its own argot, brands of enthusiasm, and ways to pass the time, offers the possibility of understanding culture at large through the paradox of examining the way it sets itself apart from culture at large. It also may help one to understand how a single religion such as Christianity could have given rise to so many strange sects.

Even though there is something basic linking all riders together, there are also as many million reasons for riding as there are riders. Under scrutiny, then, that single bond fractures into a dozen shards of intent: a delight that feels just like freedom in simply moving through the air; a desire to put yourself firmly *someplace*, so that you know who you are and have  a name to call yourself; a need to be alone and a need to come together, mixed just so.

We learned to ride motorcycles under the hot sun pressing its iron weight on top of the empty parking lot at Floyd Bennett Field, without benefit of any mitigating breeze off Jamaica Bay. Our field instructor was probably a former Marine, given his approach to teaching; first his neck would grow larger, then his face would deepen to a raw-steak red, and finally he would bark into his loudspeaker and ground you for making a mistake. It is an extremely effective pedagogical method, and I have never again forgotten to pull in the clutch when coming to a stop.

Around and around we went: first being pushed with the engine dead, feeling the weight of several hundred pounds as it found its balance between our legs; then finding the happy point where the clutch went out and the gear went in, causing us to feel, even moving forward at fifteen miles an hour in a parking lot with twenty other tremulous beginners, an incredible sensation. Sweat running in private rivulets under our helmets, jackets, and gloves on this beach day, we felt how the motorcycle cannot be steered, but it can be willed to follow you.

I went back to Tad's loft the night after that weekend, sunburned and tired to the point of being wired. I told him I wanted to go look for a bike immediately. He looked warily surprised. Perhaps you should wait for next weekend, to make sure you like it, he said. Like it? Are you kidding? I laughed. His hesitation annoyed me.

Nonetheless, that week we got into his three-speed International truck with the rust-aerated floor and went out to Ghost Motorcycles on Long Island. I had no idea what to look for, but I was confident I would know it when I found it. What I found was a studiously simple motorcycle, a 500cc V-twin Moto Guzzi, red-and-black, a workhorse, and I thought it beautiful. It was beautiful, too, in the way a dark Mediterranean villager can look unspeakably handsome in his ill-fitting polyester sweater and short double-knit trousers. It had stood in a row of similar orphans outside. Tad told me his father loved his Moto Guzzi, a reliable machine and easy to work on. Thus I was influenced in the way most motorcyclists start down whatever divergent stream they end up paddling for life: Dad always liked Harleys, so Junior does too; he saw his buddy ride up on a sportbike and thought it looked tough; she got a bike just like her boyfriend's bike. The day before I had looked at a perfectly good used Honda that was half the price, but I went home and had a dream about the Italian machine. We were cutting through fog on a curvy road, silent, sharp. I took it as a definitive sign that the severance check I had received as a sendoff from my part-time proofreading job was a round thousand, the exact number on the paper tag swinging from the handlebar of the V50. I gave the cash to Tad to take back to the shop the next day.

Next in line of reflexive actions was to join the Moto Guzzi National Owners Club, which at first seemed to provide mainly a very homegrown monthly newsletter edited out of Kansas, filled with tips such as how to replace a Guzzi's stock air box with easier-breathing filters, reports and snapshots from rallies held at arid picnic grounds in Texas, reprints of five-year-old model evaluations from Australian magazines, and a perpetual column of little adages on the front page ("Tact is the art of making guests feel at home when that's where you wish they were"). With its letters and thank-yous and pieces from readers describing with only moderately mangled grammar long trips and all the adventures they had on the road, it was and remains inexplicably moving, although I realize it is just one more of the thousands of publications that speak in code across wide distances to those who stand waiting to hear.

One night before this, Tad and I had met some friends for dinner at a Greek restaurant in Astoria, Queens, which is home to the world's largest concentration of Greeks outside of Greece. I am part Greek and it always makes me happy to be around Greeks here. I felt like drinking it all in and going back for seconds.

In fact, we all did. A bottomless bottle of retsina. A liter of ouzo sent over from another table filled with construction-business cronies of one of our friends. Spilling out onto the sidewalk on a lovely spring night, calling goodnight, happy. Tad and I got onto the 350 and accelerated onto the Brooklyn-Queens Expressway, its Saturday-night traffic as exhilarated as we; if cars could laugh, these streams would have sounded a note of high-pitched hysteria. The feeling of speed was all around me, emphasized by the wind whistling past the borrowed helmet that was too large, the air rippling my thin clothes.

Tad gently jumped the curb in front of the loft building and cut the engine. Oh, so we were here. I swung my leg over the back of the bike and lost the sidewalk; my knees almost hit the ground. That is when it occurred to me, as a weirdly separate thought, that I was bloody drunk. And if I was drunk, Tad was no longer among the living. Later, that moment would reappear to me as the point at which the true shape of our affiliation became visible, although I did not choose to view it then: I had just been party to a death wish. It is no expression of love toward a woman to invite her along, unprotected by any real precautionary measure, as you storm the BQE at eighty miles an hour while swacked. It also showed how little self-regard the woman had, how much she was willing to wager in order to go home through the dark with her arms clasped tight around a man.

My first ride on the V50 took place on the West Village piers one humid summer evening, where I bobbed uncertainly on what still felt like a big machine in concert with the lights bobbing on the surface of the Hudson River next to me. A few days later I took it back to my home in Hoboken from Brooklyn. It was very interesting riding through New York City with my mind still trying to coordinate all the requisite operations at the same time I tried to avoid getting picked off by taxicabs jetting up from behind or pedestrians waiting until they saw the whites of my eyes to step blithely off the curb. I reckon I was being saved for the night a few weeks later when I heard Tad's Ducati 860 pull up outside my window.

He proposed we go to our favorite restaurant, an Italian place in the basement of a West Village townhouse. I hadn't been expecting to see Tad that particular evening, but it was such a pleasant surprise I decided to go, already imagining the taste of their specialty, an enormous pot of seafood in broth. As I was lifting the first mussel toward my mouth, Tad told me he didn't want to see me anymore. I lowered the fork. People at neighboring tables tried to pretend they weren't looking over at this person whose tears kept landing in her soup.

From the safety of accumulated years I can now say that although I retain affection for the gift of motorcycling he left behind, I did not love Tad any more than he loved me. I would still have to admit that I wanted him never to leave.

## THREE

*He smoked in the dark. Smoking meant so much more now that he knew*
*what it did to him.*
*—Thomas McGuane*, Keep the Change

W hen you go searching for an explanation of the inexplicable, you ought to have a backup plan. Through
the winter I had one by one exhausted all my friends
and relatives, even ones as far away as Salt Lake City. The primary
entertainment in my life had become pouring a glass of Ezra Brooks
bourbon, waiting until the clock hit a minute after eleven, and placing an hour-long long-distance call either to one of my sisters or to
my aunt, none of whom refused me in the darkness and against
whom I cashed the final chit, that of blood. I wanted to replay every
moment of the denouement of my affair, viewed from every possible
angle. I also wanted them to help me definitively understand what
had happened and why, so that in understanding I could control, and
in controlling I could reel back the event and fix it right.

After an appropriate period of time, my friends indicated that they
no longer wished to be involved in my extended mourning. One of
them said brightly that I simply *must* get a cat. So I got a cat. I didn't

particularly like cats, and it seemed that she didn't particularly like me either. Bill's idea of giving solace was to sit on top of a stack of magazines and stretch out one hind leg for some licking, and then the other one.

The V50 waited through the winter and into the rise of spring in the garage around the corner, and in a spot in the back of my mind where it would chide and beckon in equal amounts. Bound up in my frozen attitude to my bike was the realization that I would have to become responsible for my motorcycle and therefore myself; in deciding to do so I would at last lose Tad, without whom I had convinced myself I was lost, forever. I had kept him in the center of my being through the cold months, where he became inseparable from sorrow. At last it was not him I missed at all.

What was I going to do with this five hundred pounds of stuff I neither understood nor rode very well? I appreciated the risks of such a situation, though I was more prone to sit in paralysis because I had no solution and didn't feel galvanized to find one. Fine days for riding passed by in agony, not the least of which was caused by knowing I agonized over something which did not deserve it.

I would leaf through bike magazines with glassy eyes, wondering why they didn't absorb me as they had Tad. It wasn't long before I realized that reading about carburetors without knowing what they did or why is one of the world's great natural soporifics.

I sent a brief note to be printed in the Moto Guzzi National Owners Club (MGNOC) newsletter column called "Help Help," which connects up people with desires ranging from a hard-to-find parts book or a particular gas tank to hosts willing to put up a Guzzi-riding Polish couple on their first visit to the United States (oh, and also to pitch in to finance the trip and provide a bike for the duration; in completion of "the Polish Project," the members of the club did so). I was looking for someone in the New York–New Jersey area to teach me basic maintenance and perhaps to ride with. My first respondent was Armen Amirian, who lived in nearby Clifton and who happened to teach bike mechanics. He believes, properly so, that unless you plan to pay a mechanic to mess up your motorcycle when you could do it just as well for free, it makes sense to understand how the machine to which you entrust your life functions, and to be relatively certain it is unlikely to drop a crucial bolt in the middle of a high-speed turn.

Armen, a charter member of what he calls Hell's Vegetarians, still shares the moral bent and sense of outrage common to the youth of the sixties, although he was a tot back then. He is thus out of place in his time, just as it seems unlikely to find someone like him firmly entrenched in Jersey's middle-class suburbs, supporting a wife and child on the pay he brings back from the stage-set workshop of the New York Metropolitan Opera.

We would get together periodically, usually while he was working on someone else's bike or, more rarely, his own meticulously gussied-up BMW boxer twin in his driveway. If my bike was in an unridable state, he would come to Hoboken after work, laying out his tools in the darkening street after a long day. I would crouch, watching bemused as the innards of my bike were laid open for view, and rapt to his words, because Armen's skill as a mechanic is matched or even exceeded by his skill as a talker. The verbiage flowed fast and in response to any situation. Dinner at the spaghetteria around the corner would prompt a weatherfront of slightly scornful comments about Italian-Americans, but Armen is an equal-opportunity word-slinger, and Armenians, Germans, and men in general were never exempt from his ripe pronouncements. Motorcycles commanded his greatest lines, however, and he would never say "underpowered bike" when he could say "that engine couldn't pull the slack out of your underwear" instead. (He declared that Guzzis' electrical systems were little improved over those of bikes from the long-ago time "when men were men and wiring harnesses caught fire.")

At the outset of a new and pitifully ill-paying second career as a motorcycle journalist, he hit upon a story idea I was only too happy to aid him in researching: how to take a ten-year-old secondhand bike—like mine—and tart it up. He talked several manufacturers of hop-up replacement parts into giving samples in return for the publicity, and so it was that my pretty but plain mount received her gleaming braided-steel brake lines, new rear shocks, and sporty adjustable "clip-on" low-set handlebars. With Armen around, I felt secure, and I could call him almost any late evening and find him in his basement workshop, listening to Dylan on the tape player and machining some critical organ of some vintage bike whose million pieces now lay in cardboard boxes awaiting rebirth by his hand. He answered all my questions with similar aplomb, somehow finding a way to fit the words *nun* and *bikini* into the same sentence describing disk brakes.

I also asked him where I should go if I wanted to take a little trip. He told me I had to go to Laconia, New Hampshire, for the annual bike races and gathering of the tribes in mid-June. When asked to tell about it, suddenly he had no Armenisms to dispense. The thought of New Hampshire brought him to a halt. He shook his head and kept repeating, "It's wild. It's pretty wild." He offered to hook me up with one of the students from his mechanics class who was going.

Bob was his name, aka Lefty. I didn't understand the significance of the nickname until I walked into the Hard Rock Cafe and went to greet him behind the service bar where he worked. In a glance at Bob, you take in his dark good looks, knowing smile, and the hooked prosthesis he wears for a left forearm. Sometimes people do that when he's on his bike and make some assumptions. This does not sit well with Bob, because he considers it not too many people's business what happened to his arm, and depending on his mood he may explain that no, he was born that way—but what's your excuse?

I liked Bob's manner and certainty; I had to like someone who says to hell with what anybody thinks I can't do, I'm going to do it anyway, when I persistently felt such doubts about myself even my choice of toothpaste was cause for dither. Bob, who didn't suffer fools gladly, would sometimes become short with me, saying with no little exasperation, "Re*lax*, will ya?" But that was just it: I wanted desperately to relax, to feel the one thing that always escaped. Meanwhile I would watch people like Bob as they moved, as curious about them as if they were some other life form. I would have liked to be able to see a problem in the way and think it an interesting challenge—if I have one hand, how do I rearrange the controls so I can operate them all on one side or with my feet?—instead of feeling this queer melting sensation, as if the air were becoming too thin to breathe. Every once in a while I got so angry at this nonsensical being who had lately taken up residence inside me that I said "Goddam you sonofabitch, just goddam you to hell" and put the key in the bike and turned it in hatred and spite, while my feet on the pavement shook uncontrollably. I couldn't tell anyone what I was feeling, because how do you say "I'm scared" on a perfect cloudless day, when you cannot say what it is you fear?

On the way out to the North Shore of Long Island, making for the Connecticut ferry, my bike ran out of gas and refused to go any farther, even though I turned the petcocks to the reserve position, which should have given me at least another twenty miles' worth. Although he risked missing not only the ferry but the friends he was to meet on it, Bob patiently siphoned gas out of his tank and into mine, starting the flow by sucking on the end of the tube. He had known me for one day.

We made the ferry by a few minutes, joining José and his van, which carried his precious Kawasaki sportbike. José had also brought along Tom, who sat sullenly in the van until it was loaded on the boat. Then he went limping, swinging his left leg straight out to the side and around, to the upper deck. He lay down on a bench and put his right arm over his eyes, while his left, a prosthesis identical to Bob's, sat like misplaced luggage at his side.

Bob and I stood in the long line at the snack bar on board, at the end of which he gave me the first look at another of his indomitable talents: getting phone numbers out of waitresses in five minutes or less. (He would employ the same silky voice he used on telephone operators who had given their names in a corporate show of phony friendliness: "Hello, Amy. What you can do for me, Amy, is charge this to my credit card. Thanks, Amy.") Then we took up posts at the guardrail and looked out at the sound as we went, talking about anything but ourselves. One topic was Tom.

A few years previous Tom, newly married, had ridden his bike alone to a party in a Long Island suburb some miles from his own. I pictured the sort of party it was, using as reference the low ranch homes with neat plantings of red and white geraniums in their yards that belonged to some of the groovier kids at public high school in Akron; the parents would be gone and lots of Trans Ams under the streetlights out front. There Tom had ingested a large quantity of alcohol on top of the Quaaludes he had already downed. So swimmingly tired he knew only that he wanted his own bed, now with a fatally impaired ability to realize how his state would preclude achieving his goal, he proceeded onto the Long Island Expressway and closed his eyes in blissful sleep at eighty miles an hour.

The premedication, while causing the accident, also prevented its conclusion in death. He was too down to go into shock, too loose to break apart completely on impact. The doctors were able to close the remaining skin of his left leg around a straight metal bar where his bones used to be, although his arm was a total loss. When he came to and saw what had become of him, he wished he had died instead. Unable to continue his job, looking down the long corridor of remaining years with nothing in them the same as he had once imagined, he filled his days with watching TV in a darkened room. After giving it some time, his wife tried to shake him out of it, but he was immovable, and she left. Now the only pleasure he had anymore was hanging around motorcycles. Unlike Bob, who never had an arm to miss so terribly he dreamed about having it back, he did not view his situation as simply another one of those things in life to get around somehow. It was a burden, and it was too heavy. He came to New Hampshire to forget, although how he could in the presence of thousands of motorcycles is anybody's guess.

When we arrived at the New Hampshire Highway Hotel, a structure that fulfilled every promise its name implied, Bob knew where to aim himself to set in the all-crucial beer supply. Our next mission was to sit waiting on the front stoop for the arrival of Steve, coming from Massachusetts. An hour drifted by while the pop of can tabs was subsumed by the steady white noise of cars on the highway just beyond the parking lot. I felt as peaceful as a pilgrim who has entrusted everything to a god who never failed to look to the care of the truly faithful. The evening also marked the first time I enjoyed the surpassing and peculiar satisfaction of relaxing on a motel curb with your motorcycle inches away and all the possessions you need also in sight on the uncreased bed in the open room at your back.

Just after nightfall Steve arrived. In his pickup stood a beautifully restored gold Ducati café racer. It had recently been put together after Steve had used the pavement to take it apart. He was eager to get back in the saddle. While drinking our post-dinner beers—I never much liked beer, but when a pilgrim, one gladly takes offerings as signs—we laid our plans for the next morning, the first day at the races. We decided we wanted to get to the track early, but we wanted a winter-busting ride first.

That night we slept the sleep of the innocent. The windows were open to the cool air that relieved the day's premature heat, and the light breeze carried a biker's lullaby as engines far and near moved through the dark, back and forth.

In the morning José unloaded the Kawi while Steve and Bob rolled the Ducati down the ramp from the pickup. In a few minutes we sat suited up on our warming bikes and looked to each other for the all-ready signal. I had a map visible through my tankbag map pocket so I could find my own way to the track in case I got left behind, which looked likely given the way their throttle hands seemed to be itching. Within a mile of our first turnoff onto a country road, their taillights disappeared up ahead, and I was happy to have them go, because I had already experienced that bizarre sensation wherein you seem to split from yourself and take a front-row seat on your own life, watching emotionlessly as the front wheel hovers half on, half off the pavement during an especially badly executed turn. I returned to my own speed. Up ahead, when the road straightened and the trees thinned, I could see the boys playing cat and mouse half a mile ahead, small figures silently bobbing and dicing. Then the curves picked up and put a copse of trees between us, and I was alone again.

The roads here suffer violent winters, which shows in the frost heaves that give you a washboard to ride. Gravel and sand lurk in nearly every corner. On a day like that one, the early sunshine and empty road and candy-store variety of curves, some long and high-speed, some tight and demanding a quick brake and hard lean, were calling a rider to pour on more and more. We were going to the races, and racing ourselves to get there.

I barely had time to straighten up the bike before grabbing all the brakes I had. Just past the turn a creature on all fours was crawling slowly to the left of the center line, head down and wagging uncertainly as if under an immeasurable weight. It was Steve. As I flashed past, I saw a bit of gold in the bushes fifteen yards in front of the downed rider, on the opposite side of the road.

By the time I got the Guzzi to the shoulder and onto its center-stand, Bob and José had returned the other way and pulled to a stop. We all reached Steve at a run.

Bob laid him out in the weeds and determined it was safe—no blood from the head—to take off the helmet. Then it was reconstitution time. At first all Steve could do was shake his head, not quite convinced he was at this mysterious standstill and not still flying down the road. Bob walked back and crossed over to the Ducati, reading the surface of the tar. A white line etched in the pavement for eight feet matched the gash in Steve's white helmet, and those black crow's-feet were the improbable leavings of rubber tires. Just behind was the corduroy ribbing of a particularly nasty passage of frost heave.

At last Steve could describe what happened, how coming out of the turn he was trying to keep up with the two on their newer machines with better suspensions and pushed even harder, when suddenly the handlebars were wrested from his control and started shaking quickly from side to side—blam, blam, blam—in a massive tank-slapper. Finally there was nothing left for him to hold on to. Bob asked a question and he said, "About ninety, I think."

It was no doubt a good thing that the Ducati was too bashed to go anywhere on its own. José and Bob pushed it back into the underbrush so they could return later with Steve's truck. They offered to take Steve to the hospital, but he was adamant about going to the track. His forearms were covered with road rash where the concrete had pushed up his jacket, and blood was visible through the tear in one knee of his pants, but nothing, miraculously, was broken.

At the track, Steve headed to the first-aid tent, where he was bandaged and instructed to go to the hospital to treat the concussion. In a bid to make it all go away by ignoring it, he told no one.

The sun was savage that Saturday, the heat rising and rising. By the end of the afternoon, sunburned, dehydrated, exhausted from the daylong festival of internal combustion and from feeling an excitement I had last experienced at Christmas when I was six, I was woozy, my feet perilously far away from the rest of me. It was hell to put on a leather jacket, gloves, and a full face helmet over the sweat and red skin, but I kept my thoughts fixed on the tiny, cracked pool filled with cold water behind the hotel—that and the inescapable picture of what Steve would look like now if he had skidded along the concrete at ninety without the aid of all his protective gear.

In half an hour we were standing in the shallow end drinking sodas, all except Steve, who sat in a poolside chair, feet splayed, limp. His eyes were invisible under the jaunty brim of an Australian bush hat that bobbed lightly every time he took a breath. The painkillers were wearing off, and his arms burned as if they had been rubbed with salt and lemon. He excused himself.

Before dinner we found him up in the room, where he sat on the bed, trying to feel better. But he was coming in and out as if the channels were changing. Medication. He needed more medication. It just took so long to roll a joint, to make the fingers work as they should. But slowly, slowly and methodically would do it, for sure.

Steve didn't feel like dinner, but the chlorine and vacation had gone to our heads. Even Tom was showing something like eagerness. We were about to leave the injured, still in his hat, to the solace of the chenille bedspread when the phone rang.

It was for Bob—another job for José's van, he explained when he hung up. He had run into a fellow student from Armen's class at the track, and had happened to mention where we were staying. That is how Rick was able to call upon someone to come pick him up from the hospital instead of going out to Route 3 and sticking his thumb out. He was lucky in at least one respect: he crashed on a weekend when the region was taken over by motorcyclists, who generally help one another without desire of recompense out of solidarity, plain old altruism, and a healthy recognition of the possibility that next time they could be on the receiving end. José grumbled but relented quickly.

We waited a good ten minutes outside the emergency room, which was to see the weekend's usual parade of interesting injuries, as well as a complement of bodies too far gone for patching. That year there were seven of those, including the results of a head-on by two bikes. Medical professionals call them donorcycles.

Bob finally came through the automatic doors leading a pathetic figure, hunched and slow. Rick gingerly entered the back of the van and sat on a spare tire as if he were expecting it to blow any moment. He bowed his head in its Yankees cap every so often; that was the Demerol talking, although it would soon be quiet and then Rick would hear more fully about what he had done to himself by ignoring the kind of certainty they drill into your head at a place like Trama's: expect the unexpected, because that is what will bring you down. It wasn't even that unexpected, either—sand in a corner.

When his head lifted, you could see in the dark the white flash of a bandage under his eye. He described how his Ray-Bans had been jammed down onto his cheekbone by the impact of the road on the helmet ("They were brand-new, too," he volunteered with a smile that quickly melted), and there was the day's second notch on the stick for a helmet's save from probable death.

The world reliably divides into two neat portions depending along which axis you skewer it. Those who do, those who don't; those who would love to, those who would never dream of it if they had all eternity. See how fast the two halves split and fall away when you mention you ride a motorcycle. Side one: Really? Oh, I've always wanted to ride one! Side two: Really? It's so *dangerous*.

Sometimes they try to warn you, as if it had never occurred to you while you negotiated city avenues with kamikaze taxicabs hurtling themselves toward any raised hand, or with the landscape reeling past your visor at seventy miles an hour and the concrete inches under your shoes. As if it would take someone who had never done it to tell you what you were doing.

But danger is really the wind that passes on either side of a motorcycle. You may go for long periods of time without feeling it, hours and days and weeks of nothing but routine and happy riding, then it chooses one minute to remind you not to forget it's there, and the news is stunning.

Close calls, calling close in your ear. There is a registry of risk carried in a mental file, the things that to a car mean nothing but to a bike call like a Siren: wet leaves, gravel, sand, decreasing-radius turns, painted lines, tar patches liquefying in sun, antifreeze, oil deposits at gas station or toll booth, metal plates and manhole covers made deadly by rain, a beam falling from the back of a truck, heavy wind on a bridge. Or a greater hazard than these, which waits in primal innocence for a rear tire to send sideways in a blur: horse manure.

Sometimes motorcyclists themselves try to deny it, as they do when they wear shorts or bare heads, as if a specially assigned guardian angel drew an impenetrable shield around them. Or they claim never to have felt fear, only joy; they can certainly get testy, some of them, if you mention the word, as if saying it brings it on.

But somewhere, they all know it. And they know it is in part why they do it: the mastery of danger, or the feeling of it.

And what can be truly fun that does not at least remind us of danger? What could make us feel exhilaratingly alive that doesn't remind us of death? In that it is most successful when you separate out the dangers it is inseparable from, riding a bike is corollary to those pursuits that never feel so good as when you stop.

Those who harp on danger are perhaps more to be feared than anything they target. We are, as a nation, in the midst of an explosion of fear. In obsessing about it, we embrace it. We promise ourselves rest once all danger—from products not dressed in layers of tamper-proof plastic or from the top steps of ladders or from the winter flu—has been anticipated, addressed, and put down forever. But I could tell you something about how fear never lets you rest, how prolifically inventive, how colonizing of a previously unowned area, how wasting fear is, particularly at night. And soon it will own the day too.

Twenty years ago the most sought-after piece of equipment on the playground was the spinning platform with iron handholds; commandeered by the strongest and oldest, it gave the weaker and smaller their first lessons in natural survival. As it went twirling on its dizzy way, never stopping, it presented a problem when the eventual desire to get off arose. Around and around it went, while you gathered yourself about you, trying to determine the safest point at which to dismount. None was forthcoming, so you closed your eyes and jumped. The sand came up to grab you in a thumping embrace, biting into knees and elbows. But you learned to roll. Now these contraptions are prohibited in most places, and you get a feeling that as soon as they find a way to make all children wear impact-absorbing foam, they will. Meanwhile, in this increasingly safe world, some guard their precious dangers more closely than ever.

Motorcyclists now fear the fear-mongers. Some of them anticipate a complete governmental crackdown, leading straight to the banishment of their machines. The most recent target for curtailment, here as in parts of Europe, is horsepower beyond 100 hp. In the past the proposals have centered on setting a tier of increasingly crippling insurance requirements, based on the illusion that one bike looks faster than another, and the imposition of "safety" features that only someone with no clue as to how a two-wheeled machine works (or crashes) could have thought up.

The industry, too, has its own fears, such as antipollution regulations, even though motorcycles already produce far less smog per passenger, fewer injuries to the environment (except by off-road bikes), and less damage to roadways than cars by virtue of their smaller size. They have better fuel efficiency (thirty-five to sixty miles per gallon being not uncommon) and spend less time idling because of their ability to slip through traffic. That said, I can't imagine a whole class of products desired by consumers that could be killed off by antipollution legislation—and if we take the care to reduce the deadly crap we release into the air, there may be more consumers still alive to appreciate the products, which would be well worth the higher price tag.

Helmet laws are considered by many riders as the first step toward eradicating motorcycles—If they can make us give up the freedom to go hatless, which one is next? they worry—but there are no fewer bikes on the road in states that have the rule. However, beyond the argument about "freedom," a word many Americans launch like a bomb intended to stop further discussion, motorcyclists would do well to recall what is really at stake.

One small inefficiency of America's periodic crusades to wipe danger from the screen is our tendency to select a single enemy and obsessively joust at it while ignoring phalanxes of similar dangers advancing on all sides. Thus of late smoking has become the voodoo doll that we hope, once stuck with pins, will take with it all hazard from our lives; and so you might watch a person loudly demand that another extinguish his cigarette, for health's sake—while standing otherwise silent by an idling car releasing ten cartons' worth of carcinogens, or while enjoying a popular snack food comprised mainly of chemicals. To me, the worst possible outcome of this war against peril might seem strangely perverse. It is certainly not the one that the legal advocates of the National Coalition of Motorcyclists would recognize as most dire. It is this: If you continue to ride in the full knowledge that you could lose your life in so doing, then you are asking not for death but for immortality. The motorcycle is a vehicle to everlasting life. And if it's taken away? Rid of the very thing that keeps you safe, you would be stripped of your magical armor and left only to the quivering fear of the mortal.

In a book called *The Dangerous Edge: The Psychology of Excitement,* I find some answers to give to the disdainful who ask why motorcyclists take the risk. First, the author, Michael J. Apter, points out that risk-taking behavior is common the world over, and always has been; if it were counterproductive to the perpetuation of the species, it would have evolved out of us long ago. Instead, it has its mysterious uses.

For the individual, he continues, anxiety and excitement produce the same physiological response. The first does so through a desire to avoid or flee the cause. The second, though, transforms the "threat" into something pleasurable. How can the same stimulus produce such different interpretations? It is simply a matter of perception. We do a number on ourselves, manufacturing an often imaginary buffer zone of safety. At the open door of the airplane, the person without a parachute feels something horrific. Strap on some rayon and rope, though, and she wants to jump. The desire is based on the sometimes erroneous belief that the pack on her back will change terror to joy. The desire is also based, deep, deep in some forgotten gland, on the thrill of conquering the suppressed fear that it won't.

According to Apter, when we look danger in the face and say, Well, sure, okay, we are in fact

> overcoming (or at least seeming to overcome) one or another of our basic physical limitations. . . . Many hobbies and small pleasures . . . involve empathizing with objects which, to some extent at least, do escape from gravity. . . . The exhilaration comes not only from the intensity of the sensation, and the risks involved, but also from the feeling that one is doing something which is, as it were, physically impossible.

And if this fails to answer the nonriding questioner, I can remind him that all things are relative, and quote the recent T-shirt that says REMEMBER WHEN SEX WAS SAFE AND MOTORCYCLES WERE DANGEROUS?

In 1979 the findings of a research team at the University of Southern California led by Dr. Harry Hurt were published. The 174-page *Status Report of Accident Investigation Data: Motorcycle Accident Cause Factors and Identification of Countermeasures* compiled information pulled from 3,622 bike accident reports as well as detailed accounts of 899 crashes investigated at the scene. The results were all that the motorcycle press could talk about for some time, and are still referred to sixteen years later. The Motorcycle Safety Foundation uses the data to impress its students in both beginner and advanced rider training.

Almost everyone is surprised by certain central facts:
- Average crash impact speed is about 20 mph.
- Median elapsed time from point of departure to accident location is less than six minutes.
- Rider error is the primary cause of over 40 percent of the accidents.

- Of the riders in accidents, nearly 55 percent were not licensed to ride motorcycles, over 10 percent had no license at all, and 2 percent were riding with suspended licenses. Ninety-two percent had received no specialized rider training.
- The most common accident configuration was another vehicle violating the motorcyclist's right of way, typically by turning left into the path of the bike; most of the drivers claimed not to see the motorcycle that was only feet away. Of the 899 closely watched accidents, only *two* involved riders who were wearing high-visibility clothing such as a yellow jacket—and one of those was drunk.

There is no question that motorcycling is dangerous, but the spectrum of danger is wide, and some dangers can be vastly mitigated with the judicious use of the brain. (Gaspar Trama, our teacher in Queens, told us he had been riding for over thirty years without an accident, while some riders can't seem to make it to next week.)

In England, Japan, and other countries, you must take comprehensive training, pass rigorous tests, and ride a small-capacity, low-horsepower motorcycle until you are old enough and experienced enough to handle more. Here, any seventeen-year-old, the hallmark of which age is general lack of judgment, can be licensed to ride a machine with similarities to a rocket, after passing a test that is largely dependent on knowing where the turn signals are. These are machines that will do 150 mph and easy wheelies, and are virtually the same as those raced in national competition. The urban pilot, however, is more often than not wearing shorts and tennis shoes, and has no clue (because it is simply not intuitive unless you spend a lot of time thinking about the laws of physics acting on modern suspensions) that in order to stop quickly, you must use the front brakes, which hold 70 percent of your stopping power, despite a popular myth that using your front brakes will cause you to be thrown headlong over the bars. It's literally murder.

There are only a few conclusions to be drawn from the statistical evidence. In order, they are: Never assume there is a trip on which you "can't" have an accident; get a license; take a course; assume that dingbat in the Ford is going to turn left into your path without signaling; wear clothes chosen for their conspicuousness. And anyone who has ever raced or been down or has a pea-sized allotment of sense will reiterate the importance of wearing a helmet, gloves, leather jacket, and sturdy boots. (As Hurt pointed out in an interview at the time of his study, "A helmet can take a thousand-gee impact and reduce it to one hundred and fifty gees—four hundred gees will give you a light concussion.") There is even undoubtedly a lesson to take from one of the more bizarre accidents on record: In 1954 in Fairmont, North Carolina, two shriners riding in the Farm Festival Parade left their bike with sidecar idling before the governor's reviewing stand. The bike took off without them, traveled fifty feet, and stopped only when it banged into the curb, after hitting several spectators.

Then all you have to do is watch out for the unfathomables.

The main event at the track took place two days after we had arrived in New Hampshire. On that Sunday, no matter how early you tried to get there, ten thousand other people had the same idea. A mile from the entrance, cars and bikes had coagulated to a standstill. As the heat rising from the engine you were sitting over cooked your lower half, the sun broiled from above. I looked next to me to see Bob shaking his head. That meant his short fuse was about to meet his need to act decisively. He unbuckled his helmet and hung it from the handlebar. We were moving more slowly than one could walk, anyway.

Looking for relief myself, I gazed longingly in the direction of the breakdown lane, but police posted every few yards put a spell on that. One of them spotted Bob, no doubt because of the way his appearance stands out. You could almost see the trooper riffling through his file of regulations until he hit on one: New Hampshire may not have a helmet law—they could truthfully change their motto to "Live Free and Die"—but it does require eye protection. Since Bob's was attached to his helmet, Bob had just made himself a scofflaw.

The cop motioned to Bob and then brusquely toward his feet. Puzzled, Bob obeyed. The man in blue continued to watch his criminal lest he do something even more heinous, which made him oblivious to the six hundred pounds of Harley also riding toward him, right down the prohibited breakdown lane. Their point of intersection was precisely four feet in front of the law, giving him a grandstand seat for a beautiful, slow-motion grinding of metal and thudding of flesh. In a second all three participants were staring stunned at one another, with no little animosity. Having made it all possible, the state trooper now removed himself, looking everywhere but at the great puddle of men and machinery near his feet. Still, his presence did prevent the Harley rider's three friends, who had quickly righted the enormous machine, from angrily picking Bob up as well.

During the trip home, along the mountainous roads of southern Vermont and into New York, Bob's silver-and-blue Honda CB750F emitted increasingly larger clouds of black smoke. It had to be put out of its misery soon after arriving home. Yet Bob seemed unaccountably resigned; I asked him why he wasn't more upset. "Well, I did get some satisfaction, you know. No matter what happened to my bike, it could never be as painful or as expensive as all the chrome doodads that got destroyed on that idiot's Harley."

I am a skeptic on the subject of accidents of any kind, and a believer in the prodigious abilities of the subconscious to engineer incredible feats. I also appreciate our canniness in choosing our scapegoats; you can't pick better than motorcycles, particularly if you own one. So Steve had an "accident"? It turns out that after the previous one, he had thought about giving up bikes. He had just had another baby, an event that often spooks riders. After what happened in New

Hampshire, he seemed set to put the Duck away for good, a decision that would appear more than justifiable to his friends, in a way that just giving up "without cause" would not.

A few years later, at a rally in Germany, a friend paternistically confided as he pointed out a young man on the other side of the campfire, "He is one of the best sidecar riders I've ever seen. Enormously experienced and talented. But last year he had a terrible, terrible accident. A reminder to all of us." Not necessarily, as I found out by talking to him myself. In a beery speech recounting the event from every angle, he finally let drop a minor fact: "Of course, I was doubly angry to have crashed just then, because my girlfriend had broken up with me the day before."

Rick, poor Rick, turns out to have been a fairly powerful magnet for accidents. A contributing factor may have been his propensity for bikes that were well beyond his riding capabilities (or, to be fair, those of most riders on the road), such as the Suzuki GSX-R 1100, when it came out one of the fastest production motorcycles available to those who felt an insatiable need for speed. He had never taken a riding course, which many men seem to feel is not something they need; women are five times as likely as men to enroll in a class.

Rick's mishaps often occurred when he was away from home, ostensibly enjoying himself on a trip alone but perhaps feeling lonely and wishing to be rescued. A couple of years after the New Hampshire incident, he decided to ride across the country. Somewhere in the upper Midwest he was stopped at a light and got rear-ended by a driver who—some surprise—claimed never to have seen him. Of course, he was not at fault. And as they say at Trama's, I HAD THE RIGHT-OF-WAY will look splendid chiseled on your tombstone.

Threats, like watched pots that never boil, infrequently come from the direction we survey so intently. I heard the one about the rider who got seriously nailed by a car. The surgeons pulled off one of their occasional miracles, darning him together in a few marathon sessions, giving the thumbs-up at last after an arduous recovery. Then he discovered he'd been given HIV-tainted blood on the operating table.

The stories mount, as the dreams do. I try to banish the dread by reminding myself of the fun to be had, and if that fails, shaming myself by testing the water with other riders: Do you ever, uh, feel afraid? Stony silence. Protestations. Looks of disgust. An article I write for a bike magazine about a moment of panic on a trip prompts more letters than it has ever received on a single piece. Most of it is hate mail. I am called sick, a traitor.

I don't want to sell my bike, which is another friendly suggestion I receive. I love riding—and although I can't say I love trying to look this damnable fear in the face, I realize the possibilities for self-improvement. The bike has merely become the concretization of the free-floating terror that lives inside me, and if I didn't have a bike, it would attach itself to something else. I would be unable to go to the grocery store, or make phone calls, or show up for work. I don't want my world to shut down any farther; I need it to open up, and a motorcycle does nothing better than propel one outward. A few years ago I started going through the travel and adventure section of the library, looking for books by people who did dangerous things, preferably again and again. I always found what I was looking for. The autobiographies invariably carried a variation of the type of statement made by Sir Edmund Hillary, the first to climb Everest: "Fear is an important component of any challenge. If you feel fear, and then overcome it, you feel a special thrill." I was getting special thrills every time I went out for a spin.

I aspired to reach the calm exemplified by someone like the deep-sea-diving adventurer Hans Hass, who wrote, "I became very conscious of how anyone who defies danger in any form is at the mercy of chance. But ought one really to draw a conclusion from this?

Should one expose oneself the less to danger and to chance? A life spent in constant anxiety over losing it would be no life at all." I return to these words periodically, as if they were something to eat in order to stay alive.

Sometimes the fear is retroactive. I do not feel it while underway, but when I am home later that night, or waking the next morning, suddenly I find myself in a rush that resembles the traffic I rode through that evening, now transformed into a dense nightmare. How did I dodge those cars, I think, with them pursuing me with inches to spare? With belated panic I get a vision of my front wheel narrowly avoiding the back license plate of a Buick, but my mind recalls the fact that we had many feet in between.

Or I dream of elaborate malfunctions, riding on a bike that is both mine and terribly strange, with controls that disappear and seats that grow too tall and headlights that cut out in the dark. I dream one night I am conquering a suspension bridge in joyous concert with hundreds of other bikes, but suddenly mine slows, slows, the slope's gravity gradually pulling the engine to a stop while everyone rides on without me. My heart dreads breakdowns more than anything, although the intellect recalls that motorcycles break as a matter of course, not as a uniquely targeted attack against me, or else there wouldn't exist those endless bookshelves of Haynes repair manuals, or the ninety-page catalog of Guzzi parts I receive every year from an outfit called Parts Is Parts, its copy replete with viciously humorous barbs against the way certain parts on these bikes were devised by cruel morons. But still I can't stop the dreams.

Cervantes described well this creeping affliction: "Fear has many eyes and can see things underground."

Life occurs both below and above ground. My mind wishes to have it one way; the people who are disgusted by expressions of fear wish to have it another. But it depends on both, as do motorcycles. Joyful as it is to have the throttle in your hand, moving through light and shadow seemingly unfettered, there are other, more subterranean reasons to love and desire these machines.

They can red-flag fear, call it out from its dark hiding place. They let us shadow-box with it, then give it the old cathartic heave-ho. And they give us another chance to remind ourselves that it's all temporary and fragile. This gift is perverse, yes, but true. Knowing life can vanish in a blur gives the most compelling reason to hang on tight. Knowing we can hang on tight gives us the prime reason to lean hard into the first turn we see.

## A Brief Catalog of Spills

Riding down a forest road in upstate New York, a couple on a bike suddenly find something landing with a crashing thunk right on top of the gas tank. The bike goes instantly down, the passenger breaking her leg, the rider beaten black and blue by the pavement. It was a deer, midleap.

A young German, having finished weeks of restoration on his girlfriend's bike, is taking it for a final polish to a car wash not two miles from home. It is a warm, sunny day. The road he rides at a gentle speed points due west into the leaning rays of afternoon light. His sunglasses are back in the garage alongside the pliers. The next thing he knows he is sitting up in the middle of the street, the bike tossed like litter onto the shoulder. Turning around, he now sees a perfectly illuminated sheet of coolant on the road. That evening the bruise on his thigh will spread to the size of a soccer ball.

Laid off recently from work, a Texan has to leave his 850 in a Fort Worth shop for eight months before he can afford to reclaim it. At least it's running like a top when he does. Less than a week later, he is slowing for a left turn. A diesel fuel spill in the lane sends the bike sideways, the rider in the other direction. Passersby help him right the bike, and he rides home. With a compound fracture of the leg. He goes into shock and passes out for six and a half hours. The next two weeks he spends in the hospital receiving steel plates in his leg.

Stopping at a light on New York's West Side Highway, a rider watches another bike pull up past the cars to sit in the next lane, revving, before the light. When it goes green the latecomer lets out the clutch as if launching an arrow from a bow. Oncoming traffic is separated by a waist-high concrete divider; up ahead is a decreasing-radius curve. The other rider, now behind, watches what happens, which seems to go into slow motion. The bike appears to slide toward the wall; the front wheel looks as if it is trying to climb the concrete. Then it lies down on its side. The rider bounces once, then is still.

In a midsize Eastern city, a rider proceeds through a green light, perhaps checking, perhaps not, the traffic on the intersecting side. He might have seen the old green station wagon bearing down from the right, so fast it can't stop, although it is apparent it never intended to. The front bumper acts as a locomotive scoop, pushing the motorcycle into the air to arc balletically from one corner all the way to the opposite. The rider lands before his machine does. He is barely conscious. Maybe he wakes for a moment when the driver, who has leaped from his car, begins beating him with a baseball bat.

*"Everything seems to be all right," Tom remarked, "but another inch or so and he'd have crashed into me. I wonder who he was? I wish I had a machine like that. I could make better time than I can on my bicycle. Perhaps I'll get one some day. Well, I might as well ride on."*
—*Victor Appleton,* Tom Swift and His Motor Cycle *(1910)*

There was the Douglas Dragonfly, the Scott Flying Squirrel, the Matchless Silver Arrow, the BSA Rocket Gold Star, various Sunbeams ("The Gentleman's Motor Bicycle"), the Triumph Speed Twins, the Norton Commando, the Vincent Black Shadow, the Velocette Venom, the Ariel Red Hunter, the Royal Enfield Bullet ("Made like a gun"). There was the Indian Scout, the Excelsior De Luxe, the Cleveland Century, the Henderson Ace, the Harley-Davidson Electra Glide. There was the Benelli Tornado, the Morini Settebello, the Gilera Saturno, the Mondial Constellation, the Laverda Jota, the Moto Guzzi Falcone. There was the Honda Hawk, the Kawasaki Ninja. They were cobbled together in backyard sheds or devised in factory studios, not only in Britain, America, Italy, and Japan, but in Czechoslovakia, Germany, India, Spain, Scandinavia, Belgium, China. Other ones have arrived by second birth through grafting, so that a Norton frame plus a Triumph engine makes a Triton; a Norton frame and a Vincent engine makes a

Norvin; a hand-built frame around a Harley drivetrain makes a Buell; Italian chassis and Japanese power yields a Bimota. The United States, which now has one make, used to have a hundred.

Much of this wild variety is called after things that fly, attack, show agility, or impress, and the names reek of braggadocio or advertising's peculiarly wishful derring-do. Then again, hype can have its reason. These man-made creations provide miracles enough to make us cocky; they are constructed so that on them we can forget the sadness of not having been born this mighty, or fast, or invincible. They make us fly, but we, after all, made them.

In their century, automobiles have done more to alter human society, culture, and economy—not to mention the earth's landscape and even weather—than any single invention. The atom bomb's potential is greater, but so far the realization of it has been limited to Hiroshima and Nagasaki, ecosystems and immune systems surrounding testing sites, and the self-regard and pocketbooks of politicians and weapons builders. The car is much more insidious and thoroughgoing, however, having touched nearly every life on the planet.

In their concurrent century, motorcycles have changed little of the world. But they require a different scale by which to measure their charge, a more personal one that registers on the ground of immediate experience. At some times and in some places, the uses to which they have been put were pragmatic and little else. But for much of their existence, and everywhere the automobile was prevalent, they have owed their presence to the active intervention of their proponents. At times, very active indeed.

The first motorcycle looks like an instrument of torture. In the "boneshaker" tradition of its foot-powered forebears, the 1885 vehicle built by Gottlieb Daimler and Wilhelm Maybach of Württemberg, Germany, is wood-framed with nary a spring, and rolls on iron-tired wooden wheels. Its powerplant is a single-cylinder gas engine, descended from the first four-stroke internal combustion engine, Nikolaus Otto's 1877 invention, and Daimler's 1883 refinement, a mobile engine that carries its benzene fuel with it. Daimler's son Paul rode it from Canstatt to Unterturkheim and back, a distance of less than ten miles, on an inaugural journey that was quite a success unless one counted the leather-covered saddle catching fire. And that was it for this *Einspur* (one-track); Daimler wanted to get on with his original interest, a four-wheeled conveyance. It was perhaps a wise personal decision: Daimler-Benz is now the tenth-largest industrial company on the globe, and Daimler is the inventor of the motorcycle *malgré lui*. His wooden vehicle has come to hold the position in the history of the motorcycle that the "first" photograph, made by Joseph Nicéphore Niépce in France a few decades earlier, does in the annals of photography. Yet so many attempts to make both photographs and motorcycles had preceded these developments—and so many nearly simultaneous, slightly different versions of the same discoveries followed soon after—that these assignments of "first" have a certain arbitrary, or at least exceedingly lucky, air about them.

Thus others before Daimler had shown more interest but less success in providing power to velocipedes, as two- or three-wheelers were called. A very early image set in the Luxembourg Gardens in 1818 shows a scary contraption balanced by the feet and propelled by the steam from a huge boiler perched ominously behind the rider; it was continuously fed coal by two sweating figures running along behind. If such a creation as this Vélocipédraisiavaporianna actually existed, the difficulty in pronouncing its name must have been a close second to the challenge of keeping it going.

M. Huret of Paris hit upon another novel idea with his Cynophère, which received its U.S. patent in 1875: just use two dogs in treadmills that would double as wheels. The sanction of the French society for the prevention of cruelty to animals was meant to quell any fear of harm to the canine motor, and the inventor boldly advertised his creation to what he hoped was the waiting country: "For pleasure purposes it is unsurpassed, and when fully introduced to the American public is destined to achieve a popularity far greater than the velocipede, while the moderate expense will bring it within easy reach of all." Huret aptly took into account the public's love of a bargain, but he didn't reckon on sentimentality's role in consumers' affections, nor did he sufficiently note the fact that he was attempting a translation from a country that ate horse meat to one that did not.

Tricycles held sway until about 1902, when new technological developments allowed two-wheelers to become faster and thus more appealing. (Although the benefits of speed in most transportation advances have been economic, with motorcycles, predominantly a leisure vehicle, speed itself is an irreducible goal.)

The turn of the century was an impressively fertile time for tinkerers and self-styled inventors of all sorts, who no doubt derived some impetus by gazing Jules Verne–like over the cusp into a new century in which technology would deliver new worlds. In the prospect of utilizing the internal combustion engine, they found a wealth of problems to solve and no predecessors breathing down their necks. The field was wide open, and anyone with the moxie to cast pistons in the kitchen, burn the midnight oil in the toolshed out back, and take a potentially explosive test ride could be in business. All that was still needed was a vague blueprint and enough paint to put the "company" name on a wooden door.

While some unlikely creations managed to fly, others more probable went down the drain. Twenty-five-year-old English inventor Edward Butler's 1887 Petrol-Cycle employed such advancements as the first float-feed carburetor. (He is credited as well with coining the abbreviation "petrol.") His backers, however, pulled out after learning that the Locomotive Acts—a relic of the steam era which required all mechanical vehicles to have a three-man crew, one of whom had to precede the machine at a distance with a warning flag—would also apply to Butler's gas-powered invention. In the 1860s

England had instituted a 4-mph speed limit for country roads; by 1929 it had only crept up to 20 mph, even though the "ton" (100 mph) had long since been cracked by a bike, and in that year a new motorcycle record of 135 was set by a BMW let loose on one of Germany's new autobahns. Nonetheless, British enthusiasm for motorcycles started high and remained high, and perhaps the challenge of overcoming silly laws was one reason.

There was little that wasn't tried during the years of experimentation, including refinements, like electric starting (on a 1914 Indian), that disappeared only to return as "new" decades later. Nearly every conceivable permutation of engine configuration was tried, it seemed, from orientation and number of cylinders to arrangements of valves and cams. Some specimens, however daffy, had at least to be admired for their elegant acrobatics over a problem. The Wolseley Gyrocar, for instance, consisted of a limo-size automobile body resting on just two wheels; it did not tip over at a stop because of the great gyroscope it also carried. Much more reasonable, and in production from 1921 to 1926, was New York inventor C. A. Neracher's Neracar, which was indeed "near a car," with a feet-forward riding position, low center of gravity, and chair-style seating. It found special favor with women.

Concerns addressed by ancillary equipment have remained fairly constant through the motorcycle's history. At the 1903 Stanley Club Motor and Cycle Show in London, a comprehensive array of accessories was shown, including the hopefully named Bobby Finders—rudimentary police detectors that were actually goggles containing magnifying lenses.

On occasion, it was the infant companies' advertising that fired up more readily than their products' engines. One fetching engraving from the nineteenth century shows a Pennington, its motor mounted on a strut behind the rear wheel, flying through the air over a canal and the heads of terrified onlookers. In reality, the machines that came out of E. J. Pennington's Cleveland shop, ingeniously named the Motor Cycle Company, barely worked and often kept the inventor on the lam, though that didn't stop a British financier from parting with £100,000—in 1880s currency—for the worthless lot of patterns and patents.

To the everyman inventors and whoever they could cajole into lending financial support, anything seemed possible and indeed frequently was. Harley-Davidson, the sole remaining U.S. manufacturer and possessor of a 30 percent share of its market, was born in 1903 in a Milwaukee shed measuring ten by fifteen feet. Moving quickly from the early adaptations of bicycles by strapping an engine onto a preexisting frame (such kits were sold for do-it-yourself home conversions and resurfaced in the late forties and early fifties with the beloved Whizzer), the Davidson brothers, one an apprentice draftsman and the other a patternmaker at a local factory, and their next-door neighbor devised a wholly original entity whose components were made for each other—even if the prototype did, as legend has it, employ a carburetor fashioned from a tomato can.

The excitement of discovery may have buoyed all these youthful Dr. Frankensteins, but the excitement was of a different order for those who rode the resulting monsters. From the beginning, critics predicted the demise of the motorbike, as well they should have. The impediments were severe enough. The rigid frames were punishing over bumpy roads, which were all the roads there were, unless they had been recently rained on, in which case they were impassable bogs. Pedals were not only vestiges of the ancestral bicycle but were necessary as starters, though cruel and largely useless as an aid to riding uphill, when the engine cranked faster than the legs could, requiring a flying dismount and accompanying run until level ground was reached once more. The leather or rawhide belts that preceded chains as power delivery to the rear wheel broke all too often, and in the rain slipped badly. Until the invention of the Gradua gear in 1907, changing gears could mean stopping to change primary belt drives. The pneumatic tires in use since 1895, an improvement in all ways over hard rubber, were still terribly puncture-prone. The rider was responsible for manually lubricating the engine while underway, and he or she had better be sharp about it, for too fast a hand with the oil pump meant having to decarbonize pistons and their chambers, while too slow a one meant risking seizure of a hot engine. Fuel was a scarce commodity out in the countryside. Acetylene lamps were often more successful as a decorative feature than a help to riding after dark.

A 1913 satire of the new pastime in *Collier's* was illustrated with the drawing of a man sitting on a sawhorse and facing a fan; the caption read, "Don't you know you can get the same sensations by tying firecrackers to your legs and sitting over an oil heater?" The author made motorcyclists the butt of the article's joke:

All you have to do is pedal until the engine goes off and then steer it down the road, missing teams and street cars and small houses as long as you can. You increase the speed by turning one handle and control the spark by turning the other, brake with your right hand, work the clutch with your left, and keep track of your oil and gasoline and electricity with the rest of your hands.

Nonetheless, the first production motorcycles were warmly embraced by those who chose, often enough through an act of will alone, to believe in their virtues. Sometimes the bike paid back the investment. The very first Harley sold from that little shed was ridden for one hundred thousand miles by three successive owners, a fact not lost to the nascent advertising efforts of the company. Besides, in 1908 you could get two hundred miles out of a motorcycle for twenty-five cents' worth of gas.

The motorcyclists of the teens and twenties were laborers, salesmen, factory workers, clerks, repairmen, and mechanics, and the occasional Harvard graduate and racy debutante who, expectedly, got disproportionate attention from the newspapers. The situation, in terms of demographics and journalistic interest, is identical today. It was doctors then, however, who were latched on to by apologists who wished to cast a flattering light on the sport. (We are lacking any apologists at all in the current moment.) A 1912 paean cited not one but two, the first a North Dakotan who

> used a three-and-a-half-horse-power single-cylinder motorcycle instead of a horse and buggy. In the course of one year he rode more than 2,000 miles at a cost of less than one cent a mile and with an outlay of only $1.85 for repairs during that time. Another doctor out West swears by a twin-cylinder six-horse-power machine. His cost is about the same, and he says he has not found sand deep enough or hill steep enough to bother his engine.

And that was hardly the end-all. Another proud report trotted out the Wisconsin M.D. who in 1927 fitted outrigger skis to his motorcycle so he could negotiate his winter rounds.

While there was still some fresh air to be found outside of the cities, motorcycling was promoted as a boon to health because of the volume of oxygen forced into the lungs; it was also said to be conducive to a blooming complexion for the female rider. But salutary effects were not likely to be the primary motive for most, as they rarely are no matter how convenient the gloss for advertising's purpose. More apt to the preponderantly working-class ridership was the reputation of the motorcycle as the "poor man's automobile." Probably greater than any practical economy, though, was its ultimate cheap thrill: the feel of flying through air.

The first casualty of a motorcycle was reported to be the Exeter man done in by his trike in 1899, but he was not the last to be noticed by the public. With the motorcycle's appearance on the roads arose the perception that riding one was a dangerous undertaking, as noted by the author of an article in *Harper's Weekly* in 1909:

> Another damper wrongfully placed on the sport is that the motor-

cycle is the frequent cause of accidents; but let an unprejudiced investigator refer to statistics of accidents caused by motorcycles and he will find that they are of very rare occurrence indeed, and infinitesimal when compared with those caused by any other vehicle, even to the seemingly harmless horse and carriage.

Aside from the fact that there is no such creature as an unprejudiced investigator, the results of unprejudiced investigations don't sell papers. Motorcycling from the start was a suitable target for the kind of hyperbole that gets people riled up. So let a hundred riders pass by uneventfully; the next one who makes a show of it will prompt a hail of scorn. The very fervor with which the denunciations were delivered, however, made them a little suspect. Could it be they were less concerned with saving the rider than with condemning the motorcycle? As usual, "danger" was a codeword that reflected more on the preoccupations of the preacher than on the protection of his subject. The way riders looked and sounded was often considered more of an offense than the possibility that they might harm themselves.

The *Harper's Weekly* apologist allowed that there had been a few individuals "who seemed to think that their appearance while motoring necessitated the use of their oldest wardrobe which was on the verge of collapse," although most riders of the early part of the century were careful to don tweed jackets and ties when they rode in town—not unusual in a time when, as evidenced by a photo of my carpenter great-grandfather, even laborers wore hats and ties with their shirtsleeves while sweeping or sawing. Soon, though, some riders, unusually responsive to appearance's sake either for good or for bad, followed the sartorial lead of their heroes of the racecourse in a trend that continues today. It was considered that racing "improves the breed" so far as production technology went, but racing duds improved the rider's style as well as safety. Surely, affecting the leather jodhpurs, lace-up riding boots, and gauntlet gloves of Italian racers of the thirties, say, did no harm to the dashing image many riders of the day wished to project.

Also at work was the crossover magic utilitarian clothing takes on when it is removed from its context. At various times bomber jackets, aviator's caps, and cowboy and engineer's boots worn outside of their sweaty, risky, or working-class applications have carried a potent charge of subversiveness. The vague twinge of fear they inspire in the ordinary citizen is due to the fluidity they recall, the refusal of the lower orders to stay in their place. The threatening symbolism of black leather motorcycle gear is only partly its kinky sexual associations; the rest is the terrible specter of the prole run amok.

But whatever subliminal emotional causes there were behind the loud protests against motorcycling on moral grounds, those on that of nuisance sometimes had a direct point. More openly annoying than the motorcyclists' errant garb was their tendency, as the *Harper's* writer also disapprovingly observed, to "ride in city or open country with their mufflers cut out, or in numerous cases absolutely devoid of a muffling attachment."

The current *Motorcycle Basics Manual* elegantly states the problem: "Given the explosive nature of the proceedings inside the combustion chamber, the emerging exhaust gases tend to be rather noisy in rejoining the outside world, and thus require toning down somewhat." Somewhat, indeed. But like some of today's offending owners of earsplitting Harleys and Japanese superbikes ridden revved to within an inch of their lives, those who fitted straight or open pipes in the good old days were not only interested in upping performance (which a less-baffled pipe does), they were also thumbing their noses at a society they viewed as having already expelled them. The fondly broadcast adage that "loud pipes save lives" is just as specious as it ever was—if you are relying on your sound to keep trouble away, you are already riding way too near a fall to avoid one for long. And while the urge to continually tinker in the name of improved performance makes of the rider a sort of second inventor of his mount and is thus a prime attraction of ownership, increased visibility (as opposed to safety) is at least a secondary benefit. Since one doesn't ride a motorcycle if one wishes to go unnoticed, it is the quality of the desired notice that marks the rift in the biking community between those who would like to consider themselves conscientious citizens and those who wouldn't be caught dead doing so.

Every editorial in the mainstream press decrying the menace of these grease-stained delinquents prompted a defense of the sport from one of the "clean" majority who was getting sick of getting tarred with the same brush. This one, sent to the *New York Times* in 1912 and signed by an "enthusiast," was as typical then as it is now:

> As to noise, which is often the cause of ill-feeling, practically all motorcycles do run very silently, but the comparatively few "open muffler fiends" put the whole fraternity of motorcycle riders in a bad light. I am often asked: "But doesn't the thing (!) shake you to death?" Yet the same person thinks it very pleasant to be tossed about more violently on horseback. . . . A little less prejudice and a wider recognition of the reliability of the motorcycle will be a means of extending to more people a very exhilarating recreation as well as an economical means of transportation, which is unfortunately considered by many to be beneath them.

Although many factors conspired to keep motorcycle sales in America on a constantly wavering graph, and the worldwide industry tried every means at its disposal to increase its market—coming up with new models aimed at the wealthy, or the small-pocketed, or power freaks, or women—general opinion was too critical a factor to ignore. Companies implored their buyers not to tamper with the stock parts; in the twenties Harley-Davidson took out full-page advertisements that called bikers who ran open pipes "boobs." The Federation of American Motorcyclists, forerunner of today's American Motorcyclists Association, was founded early in the century and spent nearly as much time acting as public relations organization on behalf of the sport as sanctioning races and events for its membership.

It would take more than crafty p.r. to make motorcycling universally acceptable to the American public, however. At the heart of the matter would remain an unsolved mystery. Why, with the availability of a cheap, everyman's car—*with a roof*—like the Tin Lizzie (whose price had declined to $290 by 1926, while the cheapest Harley was more than that), would anyone persist in riding a motorcycle? In taking the risks, in enduring the weather, in spending that time and money and elbow grease and frustration to try to make it go faster, or better, or more prettily?

The only possible answer, disturbing as it was to a bourgeois sensibility, was pleasure. It was a pleasure in which the rider straddled a machine that did nothing to disguise its purely propulsive function and that surged powerfully on while generating ungainly sounds. Moreover, it was a pleasure in which the rider made flagrant use of animal skill, got dirty and sweaty, and enjoyed it all so much he or she did not care who saw the smile of abandon. This might be one thing behind closed doors, but quite another in the public streets. When some people said they were frightened of motorcycles (or, the same thing, disapproved of them), one didn't have to go far to recognize a certain transference. At the very least, anything on which one pursued personal pleasure with no nod to further usefulness or social redemption would remain always tainted.

Yet the qualities of the machine that made it appeal to a young tough were exactly those that made it equally attractive to those on the other side of the social divide. From the beginning of the century, the popular press often carried optimistic proposals for motorcycles' use by farmers, the postal service, anyone who needed a quick and economical means of delivery (several bike manufacturers, like Harley-Davidson with its three-wheeled Servi-Car, had lucrative lines of attachment rigs), and especially the law. Maneuverability, speed—the cops' favorite at the end of the twenties was the Excelsior KJ, which at upwards of 110 mph could exceed the fastest available getaway car—and an intimidating mien made bikes instantly popular with police departments all over the country. Sometimes the riders in blue were pitted directly against those in black, and reporters became fond of the symmetry such updated cowboys-'n'-Indians setups afforded their stories; one from a 1955 issue of *Popular Science,* titled "How They've Halted Delinquency on Wheels," gave credit to two motorcycle cops for cleaning up all of California, or at least cutting bike accidents by 32 percent and making the rowdies more partial to policing themselves than indulging in lawless behavior.

The motorcycle industry was often enough behind the enthusiastic press given to alternative uses for their products, and not only for the valuable image-cleansing properties of the reports. More than one company was kept afloat in difficult times by the sale of police models. The industry also recognized early on the potential benefits in the inevitable return of war, and worked hard to prove how useful motorbikes could be in that event. In 1915 the manufacturers cooked up a scheme to reenact a Pony Express relay to show the War Department how fast and durable two-wheeled vehicles were for dispatch purposes; despite the fact that the message carried by riders from President Woodrow Wilson reached the president of the Panama Pacific Exposition in San Francisco four days late because of bad weather that rendered the nonexistent Midwestern roads more impassable than usual, the army was not dissuaded. During World War I, various branches of the U.S. forces ordered 70,000 Harleys and thousands more Indians; in England, Triumph produced 30,000 Model H 550cc machines for their war effort, while World War II saw 120,000 Matchless M20s, among others, called into service there. (Many servicemen took their first, and sometimes last, rides on army bikes while on duty, overeager to aid their comrades but not to admit they didn't know how to operate such a conveyance.)

Naturally, there was nothing to stop the Allies' enemy from also profiting from the efficacies of bikes. Mussolini, an avid rider in a nation of avid riders and legendary machines, encouraged his officials to take to two wheels as part of a general program of getting in touch with the populace: "Travel afoot as much as possible; otherwise use an automobile of the useful (as distinguished from the *de luxe*) type; better yet, use a motorcycle." In 1933 the cabinet exempted motorcycles from all taxes, while the Fascist press exhorted Italy to become "a nation of motorized centaurs."

In 1936, Germany led the world in bike production: out of a total of 316,810, it was responsible for 151,195 (England accounted for 75,300 and the United States only 17,380). Bayerische Motoren Werke (BMW) produced a 750cc model for the Wehrmacht, stopping only when the Munich plant, already heavily bombed, was finally taken by the Allies. Among the retributions visited on the Germans after the war was to take away their motorcycles, forbidding participation in racing events and manufacturing until the beginning of the fifties. BMW's leftover cylinder heads were made into saucepans.

A freelance writer searching for salable topics has had, for decades, one surefire option: the news that motorcycling has at last, finally, dragged itself out of the mud to new respectability. These stories would focus on a club's charity works (bikers as a group have long been exceptionally active in fund-raising for worthy causes, organizing countless runs to benefit chronically ill children). Or they would recount the twilight-years journey across the country by a grandmother of twelve, with plenty of photos. Or they would snidely report on a "new" type of gang, like the sixties' Madison Avenue Motorcycle Club, composed of executives, or the Christian Motorcyclists Association, whose big thrill is prayer service at a rally and the privilege to "ride for Jesus."

Holding up celebrity motorcyclists as classy endorsements has been especially popular in the motorcycle press, from a 1912 illustrated item on "Some Prominent English Motorcyclists," among whom were George Bernard Shaw and Arthur Conan Doyle, to a recent *Rider* magazine interview with Jay Leno, who actually rides his collection of priceless vintage machines. Hollywood's current infatuation with bikes, now swelled to where no leading man is worth his salt unless he owns a Harley from Bartel's exclusive shop, proves once again the town's true stock-in-trade is well-polished formula, since an informal gang that counted as members Clark Gable, Victor Fleming, Andy Devine, and Keenan Wynn was the subject of similar photo spreads in their day too.

Wynn, perhaps the "realest" biker among them, acted as unofficial spokesman. When *Life* magazine ran a picture of a young tough using his bike as a bar stool, Wynn felt compelled to respond quickly to quell the idea that bikers customarily drank and drove. "I have been a motorcycle enthusiast for some sixteen years. . . . The longer you ride, the healthier a respect you gain for the motorcycle itself and realize that you need possession of all your faculties to master this man-killer." It was another of those properly indignant letters of reproof that, because they are as formulaic as the attacks that prompted them, never seem to have much effect, no matter who writes them.

There was always some amount of down time during which motorcycle stories were almost wholly dark and sensational before the equally simplistic upbeat accounts began reappearing, but sometimes the cycle slowed greatly. After headline-grabbing incidents such as 1947's Hollister, California, biker riot, in which five were injured and 407 arrested after police counterattacks with tear gas, and 1965's Laconia, New Hampshire, fracas resulting in a multitude of arrests and injuries (one of the most serious occurred when a photographer was hit in the face with police birdshot), it took the media nearly two decades before they were ready for the next wave of endorsements, if that is how you want to characterize them.

The myopic fascination with the Hell's Angels culminated, journalistically at any rate, with the publication of *Hell's Angels*, for which Hunter Thompson "infiltrated" the gang long enough to collect lurid tales and a death threat. But the real stinger these boisterous events left behind was in the exploitation movies, starting with *The Wild One* (1953), based on the Hollister episode, starring Marlon

Brando as a rebel without a cause and Mary Murphy as a good girl who naughtily reports of her first ride: "It's fast—it scared me—but it felt good." Although *Easy Rider* (1969) had a more sympathetic view of its chopper-riding heroes, the feeling was not shared by many over thirty. The dozens of murder-'n'-mayhem flicks that appeared in the sixties and seventies (1966's *Wild Angels*, then *Hells Angels on Wheels, Born Losers, Satan's Sadists*) left a mark that has been hard to remove, reducing the biker to "bad guy" in the dramatis personae of most films in which he appears. (European and Australian films have largely eschewed this convenient stereotype, starring motorcyclists as central heroes in a number of releases; 1985's *Mask*, with Cher, is one of the few such American examples.)

This image so saturated the cultural landscape then that it is still afield today. People who ride motorcycles are frequently asked if they ride with a gang or if they have witnessed some luscious crime, although in the case of most, thinking to pose the question is similar to assuming a grocery shopper holding a carton of eggs has been to a cockfight. Not long ago *The New Yorker* contained a photo essay on scrungy men with beards and tattoos who ride Harleys and get into trouble. It joins a very, very long line of identical articles and books, and each year sees more. Not that it's not a worthy subject; it's just that it's been done so many times these guys are beginning to look terribly normal.

Although the positive stories—in fact less encouraging than they seemed, since their raison d'être was to marvel at the notion of good bikers in the first place—were an inevitable part of the cycle, they could never actually prove that some final ascendancy was at hand. Sales figures would tell another tale in their repeated fluctuations. First Ford's cheap car had its effect, causing Harley-Davidson, for one, to halve its production between 1920 and 1921; later the Depression kicked worldwide sales into the cellar. In 1927 there were 598 models for sale from British manufacturers alone, but by the thirties there were only about forty marques in the world. A post-

WWII surge was quickly followed by a slump in the mid to late fifties. Inept management finally did in Indian Motocycle, the only U.S. maker besides Harley to have survived since the early thirties (and which had kept alive the vehicle's earliest, *r*-less moniker).

The ethos of the fifties, in which conformity, cleanliness, safety, and impersonal modernity were the happy standards that helped wash away the residue of war and depression, could not embrace such an activity as motorcycling. In the sixties, however, at the beginning of a new era of experimentation, bikes were a badge one could wear with pride. Actually, the ensuing boom, including a fresh passion for off-road riding buoyed by the interest in "getting in touch with nature," was in large part the creation of a single determined vision-ary—Soichiro Honda.

Honda's first test model arrived in the United States in 1958 to a mixed skepticism and denial that was more than tinged with racism. But as he was soon proving on the racetracks of Europe in the face of equal disdain, a drive to win coupled with deep financial resources and an almost perverse willingness to start from the ground up after every mistake was what it took to achieve supremacy. That and a knack for giving people what they wanted, before they knew they wanted it. By building small, unintimidating, scooterlike "tiddlers," Honda easily hooked a new generation of riders. They could then move up to a new model, faster but still the kind "you meet the nicest people on." Significantly, Honda's first American success was called the Dream.

Bike sales ballooned in the sixties and seventies. Then, between 1982 and 1991, yearly bike sales in this country free-fell from 525,000 to 178,000.

The cause is undoubtedly overdetermined—complex economic conditions; miscalculations by manufacturers, including a paucity of smaller "entry-level" bikes and general disregard for the potentially huge female market; the fact that all those baby boomers were hitting the age of responsibility; prevailing social conservatism; the disappearance of the hidden destinations and empty roads the sport is made for; ultracheap gas that still makes big cars irresistible in a country that is unalterably oriented toward them—but there is one interesting coincidence.

In Europe motorcycles have largely retained their status as sensible transportation, and with every sector of society from teenagers to priests depending on scooters and small bikes to handle narrow streets, short distances, and exorbitantly priced petrol, they have never borne the stigma they have in America. (In Italy the practice is so universal it is codified in the term *culo à sellino*—meaning that by the time you've attained majority, your behind bears the permanent impress of a moped seat.) The sports pages in nearly every paper in Western Europe devote up to half their space to motorcycle competitions, while one looks in vain here for a mention that anyone races. The best-known face in a country like Belgium is just as likely to be a motocross champion as a movie star or politician.

To be sure, the Mods versus Rockers (scooters against motorbikes) street battles in fifties England were a sufficiently reviled nuisance, and those addicted to childish excess who have always been drawn to motorcycles continue to provoke outsiders to condemn all riders equally (some establishments in England are now closed to anyone who wears a leather jacket). But bikes are simply too numerous and too beloved in Europe for the outlaw tag to stick—although image-borrowing from America has increased dramatically. Wealthy businessmen now buy coveted Harleys along with a convincing getup of leather chaps and ripped denim with patches. They neglect to shave on Saturdays, put on a scowl, and make one believe one is going to hear them sneer, "Get out of my way, scumbag." Instead, they speak educated Dutch and madden other riders, to whom they don't wave. The argument about "real" bikers versus the poseurs has been reenlivened along with the importation from the United States of the motorcycle that is here the mount of choice for both lifelong bikers and those who would like to purchase the appearance that they are.

But if the rabble-rouser legend in the United States has persisted into the nineties, it is in a curious, transformed state. In a peculiarly American trajectory, it has moved from infamous fringe directly to mall mainstream.

Although there have been rumblings for a couple of years that Indian Motocycle is about to be reborn, an event that would be to vintage bike lovers what bringing back the Brooklyn Dodgers would be to baseball fans, all that has appeared so far is expensive items of clothing bearing the old logo. It seems likely to many who know enough to care about such things that this is about all that will be resurrected of the old marque—and that in general bikes themselves are becoming incidental to the money that can be made off them.

The miscreant's sidekick now helps sell a twelve-thousand-dollar beaded bustier on a magazine cover or becomes the theme of a New York tourist-trap burger joint complete with rigged Harleys that vibrate and smoke for the patrons, all while actual bikers are discouraged from visiting or working there. The motorcycle, as a succinct image of power at once awesome and threatening, is ideal for advertising's purposes, particularly in an era when purchasing has supplanted doing. Once limited to a role as semaphore or backdrop, however, the denatured bike actually ceases to be a bike at all.

The motorcycle's new fantasy world is carefully arranged. It is one in which eternal suaveness, animal appeal, hipness—at bottom, signs of genetic durability that stand in for immortality—are frozen into permanent availability by the lens. To enter its alluring precincts, the viewer need only amass all the props to re-create the scene. People who have no intention of ever riding a bike sport black leather jackets, the more nasty zippers and buckles the better, knock-off engineer boots à la Brando (with the addition of a Chanel label and the kind of price tag that makes you wonder if rich folks had to turn in their brains in exchange for the money), and Harley bandannas. In fact, riding a bike would intrude on this scene, introduce incorrigible reality into a bargain struck precisely to banish its integral aspects, namely impermanence, uncertainty, the distinct possibility of a failed promise, true and grave risks. Nowhere, you will note, is a reminder that the only purpose those togs originally had was to prevent lurid skin abrasions or crushed foot bones in an accident. The real item for sale in the ads for motorcyclish goods is a purely magical sensation: you get to feel like a rugged individualist while also becoming socially and sexually acceptable to a wide pool that shares the same standard of style.

In grasping this latest development, it may be necessary to recall that motorcycles have shared their century almost exactly with the cinema. Perhaps the movies eclipse the automobile as the most influential invention after all.

Film is a medium of elision. In the dark, the frames move by so quickly you cannot see the black bars separating each of the still pictures; the movie, with the viewer's assent, has wished actuality away. What is seen leaps effortlessly about through time and space as we stare transfixed. Raised up as members of a vast audience whose greatest desire is to sit still while all manner of riches are delivered to our laps, we are not seekers but receivers, and we seem bent on keeping it that way. All you need to enter—whether the fantasy world of the ad, the confected reality of the movies, or the surrogate cities of Disneyland and malls and instant suburbs—is to put down your money. It's easy and risk-free.

Near the end of motorcycles' first century, actual motorcycles seem fewer and fewer while the tidy simulations proliferate. By their proximity alone, they stir in us a desire for the featured underwear, perfume, chewing tobacco. Reduced to a stylish code, a charm on the bracelet of fashion, they become safe for consumption while lending a sense of false danger to the proceedings. Their appearance has no lasting effect except, like junk food, to provoke a hunger for more (a quality reaching its apotheosis in the concept of removable tattoos). Like so many holograms, they radiate their alluring substancelessness onto every surface. Motorcycles are everywhere today, but the hand passes right through them.

## Some Notable Riders of Past and Present, Excluding Current Movie Stars

### GEORGE BERNARD SHAW

In "How Frank Ought to Have Done It," a self-biography written by Shaw in the guise of his old editor Frank Harris, GBS wrote of himself: "He likes machines as a child likes toys, and once very nearly bought a cash register without having the slightest use for it. When he was on the verge of sixty he yielded to the fascination of a motor bicycle, and rode it away from the factory for seventy-seven miles, at the end of which, just outside his own door, he took a corner too fast and was left sprawling."

### T. E. LAWRENCE

He was enamored of the British machine known as the Rolls-Royce of motorcycles, the Brough Superior, and particularly the SS100 model, of which he owned more than one and on one of which he was killed in 1935. They were capable of a 100-mph top speed. Some who knew Lawrence were of the opinion that his death was really the result of a death wish, not an accident.

### DOUGLAS "WRONG WAY" CORRIGAN

The aviator who flew solo from New York to Dublin—after claiming he was aiming for California—in twenty-eight hours in 1938 was a Harley enthusiast; there has always been a confluence of pilots and bikers (see below), and sometimes one of airplanes and motorcycles (you can, for instance, buy a Moto Guzzi four-stroke air-cooled engine, 750cc or 1100cc displacement, to power a light plane). Corrigan was utterly emblematic of a very specific type of flier/rider: the inveterate gearhead, touched with more than a bit of craziness. A 1995 obituary described the "airborne crate" in which he completed his endearing 1938 stunt: he bought it well used and then "ripped out the original 90-horsepower engine and replaced it with a 165-horsepower model cobbled together from two old

Wright engines. He had also installed five extra fuel tanks, which completely blocked his forward view, and various parts, including the cabin door, were held together with baling wire."

CHARLES LINDBERGH _____

The hero of perhaps the last age in which it was possible to have heroes was a perfect example of the taciturn type drawn to both flying and riding motorcycles. He was an airplane barnstormer before he became more sober, at least to the public's mind; his desire to leap out of planes, as one might imagine, along with his desire to ride bikes, he "could not explain."

> It was the quality that led me into aviation in the first place when safer and more profitable occupations were at hand, and against the advice of most of my friends. It was a love of the air and sky and flying, the lure of adventure, the appreciation of beauty. It lay beyond the descriptive words of men—where immortality is touched through danger, where life meets death on equal plane; where man is more than man, and existence both supreme and valueless at the same instant.

ROY ROGERS _____

Ever since he was Len Slye of Duck Run, Ohio, Roy Rogers rode motorcycles, when he wasn't riding Trigger, that is. Long after he declared himself too old for horses, he still rode his bike.

KONRAD LORENZ _____

The Austrian animal behaviorist and Nobel laureate took up motorcycle racing while studying anatomy at the University of Vienna, but he was prevailed upon to quit as it was too dangerous. He did, however, continue riding for recreation and transportation.

JAMES DEAN _____

Although the screen legend was launched into near hysterical posterity at age twenty-four by a Porsche Spyder racecar, Dean had loved biking since he was an Indiana farm boy. The *Hollywood Reporter* wrote that he watched the wedding of what some believe to have the been the great love of his short life, Pier Angeli, to Vic Damone "a-straddle his motorcycle across from St. Timothy's." Among the bikes he owned at one time or another were a couple of Triumph twins, a BSA, and a Whizzer.

ELVIS PRESLEY ───────────────────────────

The King was a devoted motorcyclist, much to the dismay of those with a financial interest in his continued celebrity—and to the delight of the savvy p.r. organ of Harley-Davidson, the magazine *The Enthusiast*, which often pictured him astride the Milwaukee product. In *Roustabout*, a supremely forgettable movie, Presley is a baby-faced rebel who hits the road on a shiny red "Japanese sikkle" (which he rides while singing) and joins the carnival. This 1964 flick is wonderfully resurrected in 1986's *Eat the Peach*, in which the bike-riding, down-on-their-luck Irish protagonists obsessively watch their favorite movie, *Roustabout*, until they hit on a plan intended to change their fortunes: building a Wall of Death in the middle of the depressed Irish countryside.

BOB DYLAN ───────────────────────────────

The cryptic, difficult, arrogant, charming genius let a motorcycle do the talking for him in 1966. He was taking his Triumph to the shop near his Woodstock, New York, home when he went sliding. How bad was he hurt? Dylan wasn't saying. Still, it precipitated an eighteen-month dropout from the world, and perhaps one that saved him from the slower crash that he had reportedly been living (witness the previous year's *Don't Look Back*).

KENNETH ANGER ─────────────────────────────

A child actor and son of a Hollywood agent, Anger grew up to be an influential underground filmmaker and writer. He was fascinated by the motorcycle as the magnetic totem of a gay cult, and explored its fetishistic powers in a demented, campy dream titled *Scorpio Rising*

(1964). After being seized, the movie became a test case for American obscenity laws.

## JOHN GARDNER

The novelist and author of *On Moral Fiction* was killed in a bike accident near his Susquehanna, Pennsylvania, home in 1982. He had cut quite a figure on the State University of New York at Binghamton campus, where he headed the writing department, in his black leather jacket and riding a Honda 750. He was described in a profile as a "small, potbellied man" whose "white hair falls over his shoulders so he looks something like a pregnant woman trying to pass for a Hell's Angel."

## MALCOLM FORBES

Among the toys collected by the billionaire publisher were Fabergé eggs and motorcycles. He would host rides for dozens of family members and invited guests through the New Jersey countryside; with everyone wearing a vest embroidered with the "Capitalist Tools" logo, it looked like the world's most genteel gang. Upon Forbes's death in 1990, Brendan Byrne, former governor of New Jersey, wrote a letter of condolence in which he revealed that Forbes had "talked [him] into" changing the law so that motorcycles would be allowed on the Garden State Parkway. "I had to fire three commissioners to get the rules changed but I think over the years it has saved a lot of lives."

## ROBERT HUGHES

Long the art critic for *Time* magazine and an unapologetically opinionated observer of culture at large, he is also an unapologetic lover of riding. In 1971 he published an essay in the newsweekly titled "Myth of the Motorcycle Hog." He tried to define the core of the experience:

> Riding across San Francisco's Golden Gate Bridge on his [sic] motorcycle, the biker is sensually receptive every yard of the way to the bridge drumming under the tires, to the immense

Pacific wind, to the cliff of icy blue space below. . . .There is nothing second-hand or vicarious about the sense of freedom, which means possessing one's own and unique experiences, that a big bike well ridden confers. Anti-social? Indeed, yes. And being so, a means to sanity. The motorcycle is a charm against the Group Man.

## THOMAS MCGUANE

At least he *was* a motorcycle enthusiast: an essay collected in *An Outside Chance* details his growing lust for a motorcycle after he moved to California, his purchase of a Matchless, and his subsequent disillusionment from the perspective of the pavement. It is, actually, a textbook example of how not to introduce yourself to motorcycling. But it was apparently fun while it lasted. The book also contains a fine, if slightly heavy-breathing, piece on witnessing the spectacle that is motocross.

## ANN RICHARDS

The strong-minded, tart-mouthed ex-governor of Texas received the ideal sixtieth-birthday present: a pearl-white Harley. And one suspects this one, unlike the purple Harley given to Liz Taylor by Malcolm Forbes, has a fair chance of getting used.

## A FEW OTHERS

| | |
|---|---|
| King Albert I of Belgium | C. Wright Mills |
| Captain America | Jerry Lee Lewis |
| Jack Dempsey | Richard Fariña |
| Douglas MacArthur | Stephen King |
| Haile Selassie | Dr. Oliver Sacks |
| Che Guevara | Senator Ben Nighthorse Campbell |
| Pancho Villa | |

## FIVE

*The great affair is to move.*
*—Robert Louis Stevenson*

Th> here was no one I needed to tell that I was taking a train to
Philadelphia for a day in the middle of November, so I
made a slit in the face of a week and slipped unnoticed
through to another place. At some point on the tracks outside of
Trenton I recognized that I was both adult and alone, conditions
upon which one can base sudden decisions of bizarre magnitude.

I had achieved few of my several dozen declared goals in life, usually getting a tenth of the way there until the destination vanished
behind smoke and tears. But I was going to get a new motorcycle,
dammit. Nothing was going to deter me, not the fact that I didn't
really need one, the V50 still an amiable friend who rarely complained; not the officer of Moto Guzzi North America, who spent
forty-five minutes with me on the phone trying to talk me into a
1000cc Le Mans IV when what I had called about was the 650cc
Lario I had seen in a European magazine—instantly falling for its
look of compressed speed—and learned had been imported in small

and apparently hidden numbers. I knew I was going to buy it anyway, and this trip to Philadelphia to see it was an excuse to get lost inside a sense of purpose that I missed in long days of proofreading romance novels and posting poetry manuscripts into futile orbit around distant dead stars.

Outside of 30th Street Station I entrusted myself to a cabbie and got pressed into the backseat as a mysterious city flashed by. Eight dollars later I stood in front of a brick building at the edge of Old Town, alone in the cold wind. The neighborhood looked utterly uninhabited, and I knew instantly that if I were to live in Philadelphia, I would live here. The hand-painted sign above the double doors read THE SPARE PARTS CO.

The doors opened onto a small floor crowded with five or six bikes, used and new, which left a narrow path among them to the wooden counter at the end of the room. The man behind it looked up, startled it seemed, although he expected me. I glimpsed a flash of white in the passageway between the shop's front room and the work-shop, and I knew it was the Lario; I had been told on the phone it was a white one, a rarity among the rare ones shipped here. I thereafter averted my eyes and would not allow myself a look at it until I decided it was time, in the same way I had teased myself when I was a kid by insisting that my eye not return to a disturbing word on a book page—for some reason the shape and sound of the word "coffin" made me hear terror's voice—whereupon my eye would disobey again and again.

I forced my attention to the man, who was showing an enigmatic smile on his round face. I quickly gathered that he *was* the Spare Parts Co. We sat on opposite sides of the counter and chatted, as if the Lario were not the single reason for my visit; Franz seemed to have all the time in the world to talk about this 'n' that. He was only a few years older than I, with a long ponytail of thinning blond hair caught up in a series of hairbands down his back. He crouched on an antique wooden kitchen chair, which brought him up to the same height I was, sitting on a high stool. The chair creaked as he reached for yet another Vantage and his Bic lighter, to add to the mound of butts threatening to overflow the ashtray, which he was obviously loath to empty. People who have worked hard to become sole proprietor of the kind of business that accumulates oily rags in a roomful of gas tanks often develop this paranoia.

After nearly an hour I decided it was time to smile and look inquisitive while saying, "And where is the Lario?" Within moments we were back at the counter, dealing. The motorcycle was a 1987, he told me; it was now late 1988. What had it been doing here all that time? Well, and he listed all the improvements and doctoring he had done: K&N air filters, valve spring update, European turn signals, electronic ignition, and so on. I barely listened, because I didn't really understand everything he was telling me, and because I wanted to hear nothing that would dissuade me from the decision I had made long before I got on the train in Newark. It hadn't even made a dent when I got the long speech from the company man about how I *really* wanted a Le Mans, nor when I heard this bike had been here for two years, nor when I heard a term like "update," all of which should have ignited warning flares.

I had hoped to get financing through the shop, since as I had absolutely no business buying a brand-new motorcycle, I had nowhere near the money to afford it. On this point Franz was firm, but it was as beautifully draped with veils as his brilliantly low-pressure sales tactics, so I hardly noticed. Well then, I would ask my father for a loan against his pension plan; I was oddly confident he would do so for me, even though my mother was so beside herself about this development in my life that she went through all sorts of mental contortions to help herself cope: it's just a phase she's going through, and when she grows up she will give up motorcycles; I'll refuse to engage in any conversation about them, or I'll go into the house when she leaves, and therefore she won't really be riding if I don't see her doing it.

That night I was back in Hoboken, and I wasn't altogether sure I had really been to another city, in another state.

The approach of June had started to mean only one thing to me: anticipating Father's Day weekend and thus New Hampshire, when the motorcyclists returned on schedule like migrating terns. For some reason it was always preternaturally hot up there on race weekend, and whenever I crossed the state line and started to see clots increasing to streams of other bikers the closer to Lake Winnipesaukee I came, vacation recollections overtook me, sweet pangs of the perennial desire to return to the carelessnesses of childhood. For a weekend I would give myself permission to indulge every desire for soft ice cream, lobster rolls, and aimless lounging that passed over me; I would buy T-shirts and pins with little sayings on them like "Italian Motorcycle Repair Kit" accompanied by a picture of a cannon.

The New Hampshire Highway Hotel had burned down sometime after we stayed there, which I hoped didn't mean anything. Armen recommended the place he had always stayed in, away from the maddening crowds and about a half hour from the track. It was in Alton Bay, down at the end of a long finger of the lake that pointed directly at Boston. When I found out that our cabin could sleep six and that so far it was just Bob and me and Bob's friend Mike, an idea started forming in the back of my mind. Every time I had called the Spare Parts Company to ask a question, Franz sounded breathless and would finally admit that he was elbow-deep in oil and also had three customers waiting at the counter and could he call me back. He would do so after nine or ten at night, weekend or weekday. He did little but work, and his life took place in the shop. His friends saw him there, and he ate his meals there, in the form of delivery from the corner restaurant or sandwiches from an obscenely overpriced gourmet shop near the Betsy Ross house. He didn't even have a telephone at his home, a loft a short walk away.

A few weeks before the middle of June, I started telling him he needed a vacation. I admit it, he said, I admit it. And I've got the perfect place, I said. Thereafter I started calling him nearly every day to pester him, and he would laugh and say how maybe he would come to New Hampshire anyway. He hadn't taken a break in a couple of

years, except for the early-spring week he always went down the Blue
Ridge Parkway with friends. I felt as though I were having an out-of-
body experience whenever I phoned; I had no idea why I was doing
it. I had met Franz twice, once on that displaced November day and
again in April when I finally came to pick up the bike, a nearly disas-
trous rainy day when I was in a hurry even though I was nervous as
hell about this cherry machine and its unfamiliar controls. I wondered what I could have in common with him, although he was so
gentle on the phone, where I could hear him sucking deeply on his
sixteenth Vantage while the kind of music I associated with numb-
skull teenage boys played distantly on the shop radio. I could envision him there at night, in the small kingdom of his own devising,
working and smoking, working and smoking. My mind imbued it
with the kind of homey comfort I never associated with my late
nights of working and smoking, working and smoking. I imagined he
must be satisfied with life in the way I imagined of all strangers when
I looked at their glowing windows from the darkness outside.

When at last he said he would come to New Hampshire, I started
in on him to ride up with me. Hoboken was directly on the way from
Philadelphia, I pointed out. Finally he said yes to that too, and I felt
as if I had won gratuitous praise from a stranger.

I looked out my bedroom window onto the street at nine in the
morning. The sky looked like a used rag. The only rain gear I pos-
sessed was a fifteen-dollar yellow slicker suit with a huge hole over
one calf to show how the previous year, having dismounted the V50
in a rainstorm I had been running through for a while, I stood close
to a hot tailpipe while unbeknownst to me the yellow stuff was rapid-
ly melting and pulling back like the Wicked Witch of the West. One
of the several resolutions I would arrive at by the end of that very
long day was to buy a new rainsuit immediately.

An hour late, I heard a lovely rumble gathering outside, and I
looked out to finally see a white Le Mans III round the corner. It was
striking how commandingly at home the rider looked on this
machine; I'm sure the sight caused me to give the sort of appreciative

eye that one instinctively gives to any fit specimen of the human figure that walks utterly self-possessed down the street.

In a few minutes a man from Philadelphia whom I barely knew
was standing in the kitchen of my apartment, apologizing for his late-
ness and making me feel very odd that such a thing had come to pass.
I was gathering up my bags when the phone rang. It was an old friend
from my days as an editorial assistant in a publishing house. He now
worked in the advertising department of a tony weekly magazine, and
he was offering me a job writing a lengthy but simple advertorial.
This was not about art. He told me I could finish it in a matter of
weeks, and that it would pay five thousand dollars.

I had been busting it to bring in three-fifty a week, and now this
fell into my lap. Franz stood quietly in the kitchen while I settled the
details with my friend and told him I'd phone as soon as I got back.
After I hung up Franz said, "I don't understand what it is you do, but
I know you're very good at it." I felt suffused with appreciation and
shame, because I had received a compliment for something I derid-
ed. But the thought of holding a slip of paper saying to pay to my
order an amount that verged on the degenerate was already tasting
delicious. I hated everything about money, probably no aspect more
than the fact that I never had enough.

As we rolled through the Holland Tunnel into the city, we both
found that one spot on the throttle that would make the sound of the
engine turn the concrete chasm into an acoustic chamber, filling it
with a ringing reverberation so great we were riding not oily pavement but a flying carpet of sound waves. Upon exiting the tunnel we
were splattered with raindrops.

The farther north on the Taconic Parkway we got the heavier the
rain and the darker the skies. Finally it settled at reasonably driving.
The weekend's famed heat was nowhere in evidence. By the time we
passed Poughkeepsie, a quarter of the way to our destination, my
jeans under the chintzy yellow plastic were sodden from my seat to
my knees. I could feel water squish whenever I shifted my weight.
Franz, who had the opportunity to test every variety of motorcycle

gear available and then buy at cost, was wearing an old British Bel-
staff suit of oiled canvas, an article of clothing that had stood the test
of time as well as comparison shopping. But there is no such thing as
a suit that keeps you dry through an all-day rain. It will always get
you in the end, more specifically the crotch.

We stopped every hour or two for gas and coffee, and I always
headed to the rest room whispering a prayer for there to be a hot-air
hand dryer. If there was, I would take my fish-cold gloves and stick
them on the nozzle. It amused children, whose mothers were meanwhile valiantly trying to keep small hands under the running water,
to see an inflated black hand waving from the wall. Then I would
turn and direct the blast of hot air across my shoulders, where the
muscles were tensing up from the cold, moist air forced past my col-
lar as I rode. By the second stop we made, a mere finger on those
muscles could make me wince.

And by the second stop Franz and I were fellow adventurers on the
same campaign into unknown territory, every odd look received forcing us further into comradeship. You do receive odd looks, too,
entering a diner with water streaming from your clothes, walking a
bowlegged walk with rasping thighs encased in layers of clothing,
face unnaturally red.

We had left late, and we were getting later all the time; it is not
possible to hurry in a rain like that. We stopped for dinner, and when
we came outside it had become night. The rain was still coming
down, though not as insistently; to compensate the temperature had
dropped considerably. I was now shivering most of the time, except
when my muscles turned to ice. We had been on the road for over
eight hours, and we weren't even near Manchester. This was the part
of the journey where the roads you have yet to arrive upon stretch
themselves out, longer and longer, and time conspires by slowing
down to a deadly tick, tock.

From the point we got onto Route 28 and the ostensible last twenty-five miles of our journey, I no longer believed it was possible to
arrrive. It was black dark, every oncoming headlight an enemy

attempting to blind us with a vicious glare. Franz was ahead, and he maintained a steady pace that was the exact speed I would have chosen if I had been alone, which I now know is the product of a generous talent few possess.

Nothing seemed more interminable than Route 28, including the entire trip. We were now approaching nine hours, all of it in a cold rain, and I didn't know how much longer I could last. I was beginning to think we must have overshot our mark and were now a good part of the way to Canada. Then out of the dark a sign came flying into our headlights. It read ALTON BAY 7 MILES. Franz flicked his signal and turned in to a closed gas station, where we pulled up under the canopy. We got off and shook ourselves like dogs. "Man, what I wouldn't give for a glass of sour mash right now," I remarked, and Franz started concocting a fantasy about the soda machine whose red glow was mirrored in the pavement's wet sheen next to the garage. It would dispense little bottles of Wild Turkey and Maker's Mark and Jack Daniel's, and I could see it transform itself before my eyes. We were laughing like the idiots we had become, and then I was in his arms.

When we finally found the cabin, Bob and Mike greeted us with enthusiasm and incredulity; they were sure we had postponed leaving until the next day. I peeled off my clothes and disappeared into a cloud of steam from the shower, then sat on top of the heater with my flannel nightgown billowing around me from the blowing air. I wasn't sure if I would ever feel warm again.

Suddenly I was aware that I was hearing the sound of my own motorcycle, only I wasn't on it. I threw off the bedclothes and looked through the window to see Franz pulling up on the Lario. He must have taken it to get gas for me so we could all leave for the track as soon as I got up. I watched him dismount and, while talking to Bob, who had wandered over with his cup of coffee, pull a long-stemmed red rose out from under a bungee cord. I was incredibly touched: the flower was nice—but a full tank of gas without even asking!

The day had dawned sunny enough to evaporate memory. I went outside to see where I was. We were staying, it appeared, in a cluster of dark cabins set around the grounds of a hundred-year-old lakeside summer estate house. There was a dock hanging over the cold water, great hoary pines, and a lawn on which imperious ducks would parade. Our cabin, called the Dollhouse, was the oldest, and had been built probably as a child's playhouse on the estate before the days came when no one could afford lakeside summer retreats of grand scale, before the days came when such a place would have to be turned into guest cottages or sold for lots.

We headed out single-file. Route 140 West toward the speedway was ours for fifteen miles, but when we turned onto 106 toward the track we were swept up in the same surge of bikes that I had seen, and thrilled to, both years I had come to the races. They were blasting hither and yon; they were parked by the side of the road where their owners held up signs reading SHOW YOUR TITS!; they were overrunning gas stations and the parking lots of general stores and seafood restaurants. There were sportbikes and cruisers and choppers and trikes and old singles, a loud smear of colors on the green-and-sand landscape.

The Laconia area, a white-bread resort on the shores of Lake Winnipesaukee, has been host to what are now the country's oldest annual motorcycle races since 1917. (Now the event's locale is officially referred to as Loudon, after the nearest large town, perhaps to insert distance from the often rowdy past, but all the old-timers still say "Laconia.") Hundreds and then thousands gathered for the yearly amateur events, surrounding something called the Gypsy Tour, and to watch the hundred-mile Tourist Trophy (TT) race. In 1938 came the first Grand National, on a dirt track carved among the pines; a paved course was built in 1965.

The photos from the races of the thirties bear an aura of "Those Magnificent Men in Their Flying Machines": jodhpurs and plaid caps; pretty young things taking in the events from the running boards of rackety old Fords; orderly riding clubs like Fritzie's Roamers or the Friendly Riders of Worcester, Massachusetts, standing in stiff rows for group portraits, attired in the militaristic splendor of button-down shirts with contrasting collars and cuffs, ties with tie clasps for which there must have been a precise placement rule, and three-peak police caps.

But there has been another side to the event, incipient from the beginning. The 1947 program contains this plea:

### BE GENTLEMEN

Motorcyclists taking in the tour are reminded that as you ride and conduct yourselves generally, we will be judged as a whole. Therefore, our Association is expecting you to have a lot of fun and a good time, but to have it in a gentlemanly manner, reflecting only credit upon our motorcycle fraternity. And this includes your operation of your "crates" on the open highways.

To the rebels among them, the desire to make an acceptable impression was rarely foremost when gathering in large numbers with their confreres. A similar weekend rally in Athol, Massachusetts, in 1939 had provoked the fire department to exercise crowd control by firehose, in turn causing a real melee only the police could quell.

But it was the races in Laconia in 1965 that were the crowning achievement for the fun-spirited. Some blamed interloper Hell's Angels for starting the whole thing, though it's a safe bet the genuine article was nowhere near New England; in 1965 the true Hell's Angels existed only in California (clubs elsewhere simply stole the name, but eventually paid a price). California is a long way to come from on a machine with a seriously raked fork and a two-gallon gas tank.

The charge that the country's premier hellraisers were involved sounds something like that favorite gambit of police spokesmen and eager cub reporters: the local riot was begun by "outside agitators," the more exotic the better. This was the usual strategy until at last, in 1995, a New Hampshire newspaper took a new slant in positing that the source of a lot of the trouble that visits the area during race weekend was actually nonmotorcycling local kids who exploded, presumably after waiting all year for the thousands of bikes to descend on their playground.

At Laconia in 1965 there were upwards of twenty thousand bikers—the same numbers that had been appearing since the thirties—but the town was starting to feel unusually uneasy. They were sensing the presence of the invisible gas that was the ether of the angry decade, and fearing how quickly a spark could ignite it. That fear could only have helped form a more combustible agent.

A typically overwrought *Life* story reported how the bikers had posted advertisements along the highway inviting viewers to their show: COME TO THE RIOT! SEE WEIRS BEACH BURN SATURDAY NIGHT! The double-page spread, in the same format *Life* used to pique middle America with the sight of foreign bizarreries, included photos of confiscated weaponry—chains and the like—as well as one wild one, not too disconsolate, under arrest.

Escalation is always quickest on a sultry summer night. Into the Weirs —Weirs Beach, with its miniature golf, clam roll and ice cream stands, and souvenir shops, the amusement center of the resort—the traffic snakes, then snarls. Spectators crowd the walks and spill out of bars; firecrackers puncture the night. There is shouting, and heat.

When that night was over, a local family's car lay in a charred heap in the middle of the street, and buildings stood blackened. Ninety-six police officers and two hundred reservists had done battle with the rowdies. The *New York Times* fixed the cause on the need to clear the streets of menacing clots of "long-haired, inarticulate young men riding cycles bearing such names as 'Cold Turkey' and 'Bad News.' " At any rate, since both the firepower and armor of the putative (and putatively articulate) good guys were superior, most of the injuries were sustained on the civilian side. Fifty were arrested and eighty-five received treatment for wounds caused by tear gas, birdshot, nightsticks, and errant bottles and rocks and firecrackers.

The little towns' holding cells were full that night in 1965, and it's very interesting to note that the governor of New Hampshire, John King, had signed an antiriot law into effect only the week before. The decision was not a result of simple prescience, nor was it unprovoked. The previous year's events had been canceled completely because of the trouble in 1963.

Today the parking lots of the speedway are filled with bikes in orderly rows—hundreds of orderly rows, like the world's biggest showroom. From the top of the stands, with a 360-degree vista of half a mile, the sight is slightly staggering. Every make, every color, every year from 1972 on and more than a few from before then. Walking down the rows, there is a dream for everyone: a $30,000 Bimota, the Testarossa of bikes; a giant Paris-Dakar BMW dual-purpose, in shiny black and yellow; a seafoam Ducati Super Sport from 1974, reverently restored, looking so light you could flick it over with an elbow, but on the road it would disappear with a howl before you could turn your head to watch it go. The six Harleys that came in a group, all leaned way over on their long sidestands, raccoon tails swaying from the ends of the handlebars, a chorus line of black leather saddlebags with fringe and chromed footboards. Or an old Yamaha in no particular color, an ur-bike, not much to get excited about, but it goes. Hundreds of those.

This diversity is not the product of people who all think alike or look alike, but they do sort of *like* alike, and they are here for one reason and one thousand reasons. The stands these days look barely full, for they have been enlarged for the car-racing crowds. Motorcycle racing brings a mere fraction of those numbers, although one minute at the track when the field is wailing by, riders hunched low and hanging off and dragging knees and sometimes flying through the air untethered, is proof that as a spectator sport it may surpass anything we're accustomed to call "exciting."

These ten thousand fans, then, look lost in the Brobdingnagian stands. From the top rows they can see almost the whole track, which winds its way around the oval car track and up a rise and down, another hairpin turn and beyond it a parallel stretch in which they lose sight of the machines and riders for a brief moment in which almost anything can, and does, happen.

The bikes scream. A starting grid of thirty bikes makes a hellacious noise when the flag first drops. Initially the field is so dense it seems a miracle that half don't carpet the pavement well before the first turn. A gentle tap from one of these vehicles to another does not produce the effect it does with a car, sending it off in a new direction but nonetheless upright. Indeed, it's rather amazing how fast a wobble makes seriously damaged goods of a torturously devised racebike. (Equally amazing is how many certain disasters are straightened out by professional riders, and that's another part of it for these ten thousand in the stands: they can so easily imagine what heading into a certain disaster might feel like. What they can't figure out is how the guy in turn six just made that miraculous save, because such a thing is virtually inconceivable.)

At the outset, with a solid mass of machinery trying to dive into turn one as if it were a single unit, relatively few risks are taken. Control and nerve. A bit more control and nerve than those other twenty-nine are showing. That's what begins the process that leads straight to the finish. Finally, since someone must take the lead, the rest of the field strings out behind, making it more possible to witness the concurrent intensification of the drive to win, to beat both the track and anyone else on it.

On and on they go. Twenty laps, thirty, shrieking by so fast in the front stretch that the spectators who stand at the fence are blown back, can't move their heads fast enough to watch them go by, so they pick one direction to look in and stay stuck to it. For their part, the racers are so precise about the line they choose that if it's raining you can see a five-inch-wide dry path forming, and no matter how many times they go around, a mile and a half later their tires will be exactly on that stripe each time.

My first day here, all I could do was hang on to the chain-link fence, the bikes whizzing feet from my knuckles, and gape. Now, a couple of races later, I am somewhat more calm, and I can pry myself away from the racing periodically. Crossing under the track through one of two great concrete tunnels, you enter the pit area at the center of the speedway. You can't see too much of the whole race from here, although you can stand quite near one of the turns and hear the slamming down of gears and sense the hard braking just before, then see the vertiginous lean, the riders' rears hanging halfway down the side of the bike, thick knee pads trolling the tar. Then they are up and going away again, gears rising in a crescendo that seems to have no end.

Back in the pits is backstage at a play that is going on out front. You can watch the racers push their bikes into the starting area, or you can get nearly knocked down by them as they ride off the track after a race. The rest of the time they might wander around with their one-piece leathers unzipped and off to the waist, like a partially shed skin. Or a racer might come by on a pit bike, a miniature replica sportbike popular as transportation for errands. With their knees near their chins and their seats inches from the ground they look like the kids they actually are, seventeen and eighteen and nineteen, not like the deiform presences they are on the track. You can also peer into the shed while a group of serious-looking officials with clipboards do the tech inspection, a quick flurry of looking, touching, looking again at each bike rolled up a ramp to eye level. The machines look startlingly small too.

I like to wander among the crowds who are likewise wandering, in shorts and baseball caps and T-shirts bearing legends from other racetracks and other years. (The people are pretty universally white, and this realization will unfailingly at some point prick me with dismay.) We check out the stuff for sale: suits of racing leathers for many hundreds of dollars, in color combinations that lately favor puce-and-royal, or magenta–lavender–fluorescent orange; tires, chain lube, and brake pads; as always, posters and calendars, glossy studio poses of a hot Kawasaki and a hotter eighteen-year-old blonde in a T-shirt cut off just below erect nipples.

You'd think all this would be attraction enough for anyone. But the wide range of owners of the myriad machines parked out front cannot be so singularly satisfied. In fact, there are bikers who have been coming to Laconia for twenty years and have never been down the road the track is on. They come to sit in the parking lot of the Green Arrow Motel and let the parade pass by them. There they are, in their nylon-webbing lawn chairs, boots stuck jauntily out as if they were still astride that cruiser with the far-out pegs. Beers grow from their hands. They rouse themselves to shout out "TITS!" whenever a bike with a female passenger goes by. In Weirs Beach at the height of the weekend, many of the girls have simply taken off their shirts already. Like a mechanism that can't be stopped, they still shout "TITS!" at them too.

The urge to compete on motorcycles appeared at about the same time the conveyance was born. This is the same urge that has children pedaling like mad against their playmates within a day of receiving training wheels. The earliest race including motorcycles I can find mention of took place between Paris and Rouen, in 1894; perhaps it was an open-class free-for-all among automobiles, boneshakers, and gas-powered tricycles. In the next year America saw the first formal race with motorcycles entered—Chicago to Waukegan (although the first accredited race in the United States, from Boston to New York, had to wait until 1901 and the creation of an accrediting body).

In 1897 in Britain there was a match between a motorcycle and a bicycle, and *Horseless Vehicle Journal* opined that although the bicycle won the twenty-seven-mile race by three hundred yards, it would not be long before motors would reign over pedals.

Speed, in its pure form, was the endlessly beckoning challenger from the beginning, and the heights achieved so early become all the more incredible when you recognize that the more powerful the engine, the more critical the chassis. Since the adequacy of the latter frequently lags considerably behind the power of the former, the potential for disaster rises proportionate to the discrepancy. Aviation pioneer and avid motorcyclist Glenn Curtiss installed in a bike chassis a Curtiss transverse V-8 with shaft drive; its unofficial time was 136.3 mph at Ormond Beach—in 1907. In 1920, a 1114cc Indian V-twin registered 115.79 mph at Daytona Beach, and by 1937 the world speed record was 170.5 mph, set by Piero Taruffi on a Gilera. The mark lasted less than a month, retaken by the German Ernst Henne on a BMW at 173.5 mph. Henne was the holder, however briefly, of seventy-six world records.

Nationalism rooted itself early in the sport of racing, and in heated competitions like the one between a Frenchman and an Englishman at Canning Town Track in 1903 where the spectators burned with warlike fervor (Maurice Fournier, riding a 22-hp 2340cc machine capable of 80 mph, beat the pants off his British opponent). The history of racing can in fact be broken into blocks of the years and sometimes decades in which certain countries' engines took more trophies than any other's: the French, British, and Americans tossed the wins back and forth in the century's first couple of decades; in the 1930s, England's Norton machines seemed invincible; the Italians fought back hard and often successfully in the latter part of that decade, while right before the Second World War, BMW looked poised to steal the lead. The end of the fifties marked the end of the golden age of British bikes, by which time Italy had become a star once more, notably with Guzzi and Gilera. At the beginning of the sixties the products of the manufacturer MV (Meccanica Verghera) Agusta, the rich child of Count Domenico Agusta, blasted to win after win all over the Continent: they won world championships in 1958, 1959, and 1960 in the 500cc, 350cc, and 250cc classes. (The only one they didn't win, in fact, was the sidecar competition, which had always belonged to BMW.) Such a brief but brilliant flame is destined to be remembered and mythologized; it helps that the Agustas are among the most beautiful motorcycles ever built. (My friend Wolf Knapp a few years ago penned a rock song called "MV Agusta," which was recorded by the band Antietam; the title has no relationship to the lyrics, in true art-rock style, but he knew it was a great thing to call a song.)

The decades of Japanese supremacy began in 1961, when one of the most famous motorcycle racers of all time, Mike Hailwood, piloted a privately entered Honda to the 250cc world championship. It took the Japanese just one year to erase the opposition: in 1962 they set sixteen new records in twenty-five races, and placed first in all of them. It seemed their sovereignty would have no end, and then came the beginning of the nineties, when the Italian firm of Ducati reappeared on the world scene with its startlingly powerful red superbike racers.

Road racing is the best-known and most glamorous type of motorcycle competition, evolving from the first races held on closed circuits. The earliest of these was probably 1904's International Cup Race organized by the French Auto-Cycle Club, at which cheating was rampant. The next year things were under somewhat better control at the race in Dourdan, making it the first contest of true consequence. Three riders were able to avoid the malfunctions and crashes that were a matter of course and finished: Victor Wondrick of Austria on a Laurin-Klement, who came in first; Joseph Guippone of France, second on a Peugeot; and a French rider named Demester, who was disqualified for changing a wheel.

But racing is prodigiously variegated, and people who like to compete have found different sorts of challenges in the unlikeliest of quarters. There have been, and sometimes still are, races on sand, dirt ovals, grass, ice (using evilly studded tires to achieve the most extreme lean angles in all of racing), and hilly countryside. There is

drag racing, which stands as proof that someone, somewhere, is willing to fit almost anything into a two-wheeled frame and then lie on
top of so many cylinders that he can barely reach the handlebars;
eight seconds later he will cross the finish line at 185 mph, provided
nothing goes wrong. There are endurance races run around the clock
(most often on racetracks, but occasionally on public roads, such as
America's Iron Butt, where finishers can average over a thousand
miles a day for eleven days straight); races against the clock; hill-
climbs; acrobatic maneuvers called observed trials, in which riders
slowly negotiate seemingly impassable rocks and rills; and speedway
racing, which was developed in Australia and brought to England in
1928 by "Sprouts" Elder, a name that merits repeating.

The earliest "scramble," a point-to-point competition over rough
terrain, was the Southern Scott Scramble, held in 1924 on England's
Camberley Heath. "The survival of a medieval custom whereby the
young men of the district disguised themselves with mud and tor-
tured each other" was the way British scrambles of the forties were
described by one participant; the frantically spinning rear wheels of a
tight cluster of bikes on the same soggy patch of ground can throw a
lot of mud. Scrambling could also be described as a mix of riding and
flying as well as excavating, since competitors spend considerable
time airborne, the result of being launched off hillocks at full throttle. Scrambles are a forerunner of the type of race called motocross,
which is one of America's most populist sports and one of Europe's
most popular. Children on tiny dirt bikes are sometimes encouraged
to start going at each other as well as the bumps at the age of four,
and their parents get as fixed on their success as parents of Little
Leaguers. In the United States, motocross is further refined into the
championship series called supercross, held at indoor arenas into
which tons of dirt have been dumped. The spectacle is often sweet-
ened for the audience by adding a monster truck event to the ticket.

Early track races in America were organized by the American
Motordrome League, which was composed of teams that traveled to
matches. They took place on board tracks of three-quarters of a mile,

steeply banked at 58 degrees, and bikes would go as fast as 90 mph on them. The surface was roughened, as polished wood would have provided no traction, although it would have been a lot nicer to fall on, avoiding the kind of splinters it hurts the brain to imagine. But the boards would quickly get oil-slicked or broken, and riders would become dizzy from circling sideways in one direction on such a short, banked track. The races were more spectacle than competition, and the frequent spills were an integral part of the attraction, even as their outcomes soon prompted a great outcry against the "murder-dromes." At one race on September 8, 1912, two riders and six spectators were killed; at the inquest it was proposed that motorcycle racing be abolished.

Only board racing would vanish—there was too much thrill in going all-out on these speed machines for anyone to consider stopping. In the early years, records were set at a phenomenal pace—in 1912, forty-three world records were posted, however briefly they stood—and the kind of men who raced to notch them became champagne-soaked heroes. In the week before he got on a transatlantic ship to go meet a British challenger at the legendary Brooklands track in Surrey in 1911, Jake de Rosier set three world records on his Indian (and he and his American iron continued the streak at Brooklands by beating Charlie Collier on a Matchless).

The story of one of the most memorable of these unstoppable men, Erwin G. "Cannonball" Baker, is inseparable from those of the upstarts who quickly took his records away nearly as often as he kept them for a while. His 1914 record for a Los Angeles–New York run of 3,379 miles in eleven days, twelve hours, and ten minutes was shortly bested by twenty-one-year-old Allan Badell, who clipped 3,296 miles in seven days and 16.25 hours. Baker's record for the Three-Flag Route (Blaine, Canada, to Tijuana) was broken by Ray Artley, 1,667 miles in three days, twenty-five minutes. And Baker's twenty-four-hour board track record soon fell, too, to a guy named Wells Bennett. But what Cannonball Baker had learned while throwing himself into any and every attempt always stood him in good stead, as when he was called upon to ride three far-flung legs of the 1915 "Pony Express" relay to the Panama Pacific Exposition; he knew the cross-country dirt roads of America better than anyone, so the organizers paid to put him on a train and deliver him wherever he was needed most.

Perhaps the way to determine true-bloodedness in a self-proclaimed motorcycling aficionado is to say the words "Isle of Man." If they mean nothing more than an island in the Irish Sea, the passion may only be professed.

The TT held annually on the Isle of Man since 1907 is considered nothing short of the ultimate motorcycle race. Its course winds for 37¾ miles (three different courses were previously used) through narrow streets of towns, up and down hills, around curves that kill, across bridges, past farms and high stone walls and devious vegetation. It equally tests human skill and mechanical quality. Failures can have a steep fee. In its history, over one hundred riders and spectators have paid with their lives.

The genesis of the race derived from two situations: the persistence of cheating at the 1906 International Cup, which the British refused to tolerate any further, and the fact that any home-soil competition would have to get around those terribly restrictive public road speed limits. Harry Collier, Sr., founder of Matchless Motorcycles and father of the renowned riders Harry and Charlie, suggested the Isle of Man, already the site of automobile contests since it was willing to close its roads to the public for an event. The Englishman Marquis de Monzilly St. Mars offered a trophy, and the race was on.

Nearly every year the race was run brought new legends, new tales of daring and excellence and endurance. Lap speeds rose and rose, although it seemed certain there would have to be an end, put there by the insolvency of sharp curves and steep drops. In 1920, the record belonged to George Dance and his Sunbeam: 55.62 mph. In 1927,

Stanley Woods upped the ante to an amazing 70.9 mph on his Norton. Woods swept past another milestone in 1935, when he won both Lightweight and Senior titles on Guzzis, setting new lap records into the bargain. Still the records climbed: in 1938 a twin-cam Norton turned a 91-mph lap, a figure that stood until 1950. Now the record is over 123 mph, and it is as certain as it is unbelievable that someone will top it sooner or later.

But the Isle of Man is less about records than the men who dare to set them. The perverse and determined and half-insane people who race motorcycles at the upper limits of competition are the real spectacle.

In the *New York Times* of June 29, 1913, there appeared an article under the headline "Motor Cyclists Always in Danger" (its subhead explained, "They Are in Clutches of Speed Mania and Get Paid Well for It"). Racers are engaged in such a desperate pursuit that not even Lloyd's would write a policy on them, the article maintained.

> These bike riders are not the daredevil, death-defying citizens that they appear to be. They are quiet, unassuming men, who go to extremes of care and safety. Sure, they don't always succeed, but it isn't their fault. Fate plays an important part in their lives. . . . Motor cyclists eat and sleep and talk like other folks, but at times they can't help feeling that they haven't as long to live as the ordinary man. And they are right. They are a fearless lot, brave enough to wear their lives on their sleeves, and have nerves as unimpressionable as flint.

American-style dirt track racing, originally on horse track ovals, was no less dangerous than any other permutation of the sport. Fred Ludlow, a Harley racer in the twenties, recalled the risks in an interview by Phil Schilling, author of *The Motorcycle World*: "In the heavy dust of some of the old tracks all we had to follow was the blue exhaust of the fellow ahead. . . . During one race a fellow went through the fence and was killed. We never missed him until after the race, when we were packing up our equipment and happened to count noses, we found him and his machine on the far side of the track, outside the fence. The spectators had long since gone."

But ask any racer why they do it, and you are likely to get what is termed a shit-eating grin in response: There is no feeling like it on earth. After the sleepless nights and the sweat, there is time compressed and crystallized, a pure rush, sex on speed. One has to suspect nothing but such compelling cause when so many racers are blurring down the course wearing splints, bandages wrapped tight to keep the swelling out of the way, broken ribs and foot bones, and disregarding doctors' advice and, on occasion, threats. Getting back into the ring is the only thing that matters, and most people would hardly believe the sacrifices made to do so. Grand Prix racer Wayne Rainey fell in practice before the 1992 season, injuring a hand that might have healed but not in time for the first race; instead, he had a finger amputated so he could compete. The next year his colleague Kevin Magee, with a similar injury, made exactly the same choice. Just before participation in the Mille Miglia claimed his life, the Marquis of Portago, a celebrated automobile racer of the twenties, confirmed, "Racing is a vice and, as such, extremely hard to give up."

Steve McQueen, a man who could do pretty much anything he wanted and frequently did, racing cars and flying planes, loved motorcycles best. (It shows, and you can see it, in the happy footage of McQueen in Bruce Brown's 1971 motorcycle documentary *On Any Sunday*; it is a film that has never been surpassed as a paean to the joys of the sport.) The movie star entered races under the name Harvey Mushman, and although his handlers were none too thrilled, no one could stop him. It was reportedly his idea to write the exhilarating cross-country cycle chase into *The Great Escape*, and for once his riding—an activity he enjoyed so much he also stood in for the pursuing Nazi cyclists—was sanctioned by Hollywood.

McQueen exemplifies the typically laconic attitude of the pure racer. "When you race cycles, you take spills, 'cause you're out there twisting the tiger's tail," he is quoted as saying in William F. Nolan's biography. During the Pacific West Coast Championship Scrambles "there was this big pile-up in the fourth lap, and in avoiding the tangle I hit a tree, split my mouth open, and knocked some teeth loose. But I was okay. I got back into it and won." In 1964 he was chosen to compete in the International Six-Day Trials, the most important, and unbelievably grueling, cross-country race in the world. He raced flat-out in the timed trials but got clipped and took a flier, banging himself up and his bike worse. Unfortunately it was beyond the limits of repair, per the rules, using only the tools carried on the bike.

Without referring specifically to cycle racing, a crewmember who worked with McQueen on *The Sand Pebbles* came close to defining the personality type that is perhaps preeminent on tracks and courses the world over. "In his private life you get the impression that he is trying to speed up time, to get into the next hour without quite living out the present one."

It is tempting to think of world-class racers as made of material other than flesh and bone. The great ones are great in a way that is resistant to explanation. You appreciate them not with your brain but with that unnamed center of the gut that knows without thinking how to read the poetry of extremity.

In 1965, Honda signed Mike Hailwood, the good-looking son of a wealthy British businessman, away from MV Agusta, in order to put the cinch on the 500cc class for good. But his bad luck that year had a mean twist, for he was beaten by his former employer and Agusta's next great rider, Giacomo Agostini. The Italian upstart showed unusual courage and flair, and Hailwood recognized an opponent worth gunning for. In 1967, at the Dutch TT, a crowd of 150,000 got their money's worth. Hailwood used everything he had to stay on Agostini's tail through every lap. Then, at the last opportunity, he moved ahead, as if he had finally gathered the strength to pull himself hand over hand up the rope that dangled him over a cliff. He won by five seconds. He was so exhausted he had difficulty getting off his bike, and they had to delay the award presentation until he could get himself up the dais steps. (Like "Mike the Bike," "Ago" came from wealth and had a charismatic public persona. But the Italian exuded the scent of sex in a way that only an Italian can, and he had the devastating handsomeness to back up the promise. A 1967 *Sports Illustrated* article on him was apparently quite aptly titled "Viva! But Hide Your Women.")

In a biography of Hailwood written by his friend Ted Macauley, the racer recalled the dark events of 1962.

> Tom Phillis was killed trying to keep up with Gary Hocking and me in the Junior TT. His Honda was underpowered and handled badly, and what he lost in speed he tried to make up with sheer riding skill and daring. Tom's death upset Gary so much he decided to retire from motor-bike racing. He was inconsolable. He cleared off back home to Rhodesia to try and forget. Then he made up his mind to try his hand at car racing, and he was killed practising for a race. It was grimly ironic that having quit bike racing because it was far too dangerous he should be killed in a racing car.

Hailwood's own fears ran not to getting hurt or killed but to getting stitches. "Whenever I fall off, the first thing I do when my head stops spinning is to give myself an examination. I gingerly prod round as many parts as I can comfortably reach, and I think, 'Oh God, don't let there be anything wrong that might need stitching up.'" He might have done better to pay attention to the grim irony he had already noted, as he was killed in a car wreck on a public road in 1981.

Perhaps the perverse insistence of world-class racers to continue their high-speed chases despite pain, exhaustion, and the ever-present shadow of death can be explained by the fact that if they make it to the Grand Prix circuit, the money is quite all right as long as you keep accumulating enough points, and you can be guaranteed your choice of a terribly pretty young wife. But what can explain the thousands of privateers and club racers who go into hock for the privilege of going to the track and exhausting themselves without benefit of much company or any reward?

Once again the responses fall along the same inarticulate line: It's addictive; I can't explain; I've never felt like that before. "That one minute of total focus . . ." offered one man who had competed in a little amateur motocross when he was younger.

Or maybe it's simply to gather good stories. That man, Scott Emmons, now a commodities trader and mechanical jack-of-all-trades, was telling me about his exploits over a beer at the noisy, dark, and manly Raccoon Lodge, the kind of place most suitable to such accounts.

I had been riding dirt bikes since I was thirteen, in Missouri. When I was twenty-one I decided to take a break from college and began driving trucks. I was living at home and making a lot of money, so I bought a Suzuki RM 125. I wanted to race it. But my parents were completely against the idea—their reasons were the usual stereotype bullshit, even though it's really safer than football.

I decided to enter a Friday-night race anyway in Kansas City, run under lights. On Thursday night I stole the keys to the van my mom used for work and loaded the bike in the van.

I had become a pretty good racer, after the start, that is, and at this late age I really needed a win. But I was totally out of my class that night. I came off the line and stuck on the throttle. It was a tight track, but I made the first turn okay. Then came a flat-track-style turn followed by two jumps—a hobble and a big one. I made the first lap just fine. I gassed it on the long straight and again made the first jump, shifting in midair. Then onto the camelback hump I accidentally hit the gas. I was soaring through the air so out of control I landed fifteen feet later, in the middle of the *next* turn—right on top of the gas tank. Suddenly the announcer calls out, "Who is number 776?"

The only thing I could do was hit the gas again, and now the announcer locks on to me: "He's looking pretty wild!" The next time I come around to the first turn I launch myself again, but this time I'm flying off the back, and my pants get caught on the back fender. The announcer shouts: "Oh my God." I don't know how I saved it, but I got back on the seat somehow and didn't go down. It was the first time ever I didn't get lapped in a race.

We talked on the phone every day, sometimes several times. On most Friday mornings, I wheeled the bike out of the garage, strapped on my saddlebags containing whatever work I had to do over the weekend, and headed for the New Jersey Turnpike. Exactly two hours, ninety miles, 2.09 gallons of gas, $3.10 in tolls, and many thoughts later I would turn onto Vine Street. Franz would sometimes be outside, washing or tuning a bike, and although I knew he had heard me coming for at least four blocks, he wouldn't look up until I had pulled the Lario onto the centerstand, taken off my helmet, and come over to stand next to him. Then he would turn his eyes to me with a little smile and say softly, "Well, well."

My motorcycle was very happy to be home. Franz would pull her up onto the lift in the back room and instruct me on whatever minor dismantling needed to be done. It was not lost on me that one trouble I had had working on my bikes at home was not having the proper tools; in Philadelphia I first felt the silken weight of a Snap-on tool, a true joy to hold. Once Franz looked over as I was extracting the oil filter from the bottom of the sump during an oil change, saw my right hand under a river of black oil, and said, "You mean to tell me you haven't figured out how to pull a Guzzi's filter and keep your hands completely clean?" Damn, I thought; changing the oil is about the only thing I know how to do well, and now he tells me I don't. A few minutes later I came to my senses. I was such an easy mark. "There's no way to do it, you liar." He guffawed through his nose as he ran up front to avoid the dirty shop rag coming his way.

If the weather was nice, I sat on a concrete block outside the shop doors and worked. A lot of the time I just stared off over the parking lot across the street, beyond which seemed to be a breathtaking nothingness, with a pleasant melancholy to match; the sound of traffic on the Ben Franklin Bridge provided a distant melody that suffused all time there with the longing to move. I wasn't at all sure what I was doing with Franz: essentially we came from different universes. Because we lacked a common language based on the things that had always been my referents, like what you learn in college or books or old movies, I tried to make one up as we went along.

Perhaps that was why I felt as if I didn't quite belong there, that I borrowed someone else's life when I was in Philadelphia, someone whose only job was to feel miraculously unencumbered by the usual vague unhappiness, to entertain herself, to go off shopping to South Street (I would never permit myself to aimlessly wander through stores in New York; I felt that every moment here must be devoted to work and worry), to muse pleasantly about where we should go for dinner, because every night we were able to be together seemed a night to celebrate. Although I lived in the middle of a riotous variety of the world's cuisines, it was in Philadelphia that I first, and last, tasted Mongolian food. On impulse I bought a black hat with a wide brim, the most becoming hat I've ever had. Once a week I untied the moorings that kept me bound to who I thought I was, and discovered that I could sail even though I had neglected to take any soundings.

On Sundays we'd take a ride, to Bucks County, or to Delaware, or out the Main Line, or through Pennsylvania Dutch farm country. We would stop wherever we had the notion, stretching out on grass or getting a meal that would invariably end with pie. I dreaded the Sunday-night ride back up the turnpike, primarily because it was the end of holiday, and because I knew I would find myself waiting in the small cold-water flat at the end of the road, just after exit 14C.

That summer was unlike any other in many regards, but mostly for the absence of all anxiety about the safety of myself, in the extended form of my motorcycle. I did not have one breakdown dream, one moment of panic before I set out for a ride that something terrible would happen to my bike, stranding me alone, where I would be forced to confront the implacable truth that I felt certain would scold me: You did well to fear, because you are incapable of taking care of yourself.

Oh, how happy we were.

A RALLY PRIMER

Rallies perform the same function for far-flung motorcyclists as county fairs do for rural locales, and in several ways they are as anachronistic. For the most part they are mild bacchanalia, still vaguely rooted in seasonal pagan celebration. With their gentle spirit of noncompetitive competition—the cheap plaques and prizes, the poker run or other games—they seem pulled from the past, from what people persist in calling "a simpler time." (Then again, I hear BMW rallies can get a bit razor-edged on the competition issue.)

Although there are a few gatherings that attract numbers into the tens of thousands—Americade, at Lake George in June, for "touring" motorcyclists; Bike Week in Daytona, for the late-winter races; the strictly commercial enterprises held in giant hotel parking lots in various parts of the country by *Rider* magazine; the Black Hills Classic in Sturgis, North Dakota, the granddaddy of them all, heavy on the Harleys and working-class mayhem—the majority of rallies are club-oriented and small, and have the cast of parish picnics.

If the glue that binds is Italian-made, there is sure to be more than one person cruising the rally site wearing a sweatshirt that states VIVERE PER MONTARE, MONTARE PER VIVERE ("Live to Ride, Ride to Live"), and it is not to be taken as a joke. Nor is the related sentiment expressed by one Moto Guzzi owner who affixed large bas-relief dinner forks to the side covers of his bike over the legend MANGIERE PER MONTARE, MONTARE PER MANGIERE ("Eat to Ride, Ride to Eat"). The pleasures of long-distance riding are inextricable from those of eating, and one heightens the other. It is partly a trick the psychologists call "excitation transfer," which makes even the raggedest diner chow seem exquisite, and you can eat lots, too, so

long as you get back on the bike and let the wind and cold and
stress of constant watchfulness burn it up for you.

For people who long to be with other like-minded people, in
however large or small a dose, rallies fit the bill. They become
highlights on the calendar; goals; purposes; small pleasures. The
rarest of them, like the Elephant rally near Germany's Nürburgring, add the inclusionary element of having to withstand hardship
in order to participate; it is a campout held in the winter snow,
originally a nostalgic postwar get-together for German army sidecar
riders who had cut their teeth on the Russian front. But all of these
confabs engender a sense of belonging, and if that sounds too senti-
mental, just don't say it.

One Labor Day weekend I happened to be in Watkins Glen,
New York, at the same time the town was hosting a BMW rally. I
felt left out, but not because of any show of brand exclusivity. I
would have been as welcome on a Guzzi as on a Beemer. No, it was
that I was there in a car. I had rendered myself invisible, become
just another body taking up a seat in a restaurant. I wished I could
cross over the divide; I was aching with longing to do it. But I could
not in my current guise share the exultation they felt when they
came in from the dark rain and saw others like them who had made
it to the warmth too, saw others like them to whom they nodded
and smiled, but not to people like me. I heard the talk all around
me while held off from being able to speak or laugh in response. A
man at another table was saying to his riding partner, sharing mysteries in a way I had done so often myself, "Did you see that, just as
we turned onto 28? It hit me in the arm—I thought it was a potato!" She broke into peals of knowing laughter.

The ability to feel togetherness, of course, relies on positing an
Other who remains outside the group. It can easily become the
source too of snobbery or even hatred. For the Europeans who
have recently descended on the Isle of Man during the annual races,
that enemy is summed up in one word: Volvo. The crowd would

ruthlessly taunt the driver of any such Swedish car. One rider explained to a reporter for the *Guardian*, "It's in the DoT report. Volvos have been involved in more accidents with bikers than any other make of car."

Well, we are all affiliated with something. You're an Elk. You're a Muslim. You root for Ole Miss. Your country right or wrong. You're a biker.

One of the strangest, and maybe most delightful, gatherings in the East takes place every August in Port Clinton, Pennsylvania. Port Clinton, a good forty miles from anywhere so long as Allentown fits your idea of somewhere, has two major retail businesses. One is a store that specializes in peanuts and is, to no surprise, called the Peanut Store. The other is the U.S. importer of Moto Morini motorcycles, an Italian marque that first appeared in 1937 out of a small factory in Bologna. The Herdan Corporation of Port Clinton is solely responsible for the fact that many pasty-faced, bearded young men are currently running around rural central Pennsylvania on bikes whose lineage is most noted for a string of successes on Europe's World Championship road racing circuit in the mid-fifties. Happily for them, these riders are primarily mounted on the most hideous-looking machine ever turned out of Italy, the Morini Excalibur, which came in a grape-candy hue and was conceived to finagle a cut of the sizable market for pseudo-chopped cruisers. Therefore they do not give themselves away as witty riders of exotica, since their bikes are actually monuments to pure American-style tastelessness.

The last Morinis came through U.S. customs around 1990, but that has not stopped Port Clinton from still attracting a couple hundred riders of old and new European bikes, including Triumphs and Harleys both chopped and not, and other local guests, for one summer Sunday every year. The rest of the crowd arrives in pickups and Chevrolets and the occasional Alfa-Romeo, dozens of tots and blue-haired grandmas and young mothers and urban swells, to complete the most diverse mix of people you could hope to encounter on the same country acre.

The very air surrounding the solid log cabin on a hill with a long view into the distance of trees and fields seems chronologically different from the air one is used to breathing. It is older, appropriately more fertile. A motorcyclist who earlier in the day left the acrid atmosphere of the biggest city on the East Coast and arrived here to pitch a tent by the edge of the vegetable patch (well away from the muddy chicken pens set back in the woods) might wake up the next morning to find that the squash vines had crawled out during the night, crossed several inches of lawn, and begun to spiral up the tent's ropes.

The origin of the shindig, which is familiarly referred to as Hermy's (as in "Are you going to Hermy's this year?") after its host, Herdan owner Herman Baver, is Hermy's birthday. But few know that, and the main reason the bikers come, some from several hours away, is for the food.

Two kettles large enough to stew a couple of men apiece have been sending up smoke since the day before; one holds bean soup flavored with ham, the other a turtle soup whose main ingredient until recently walked the earth nearby. Yet another large pot holds corn on the cob. On a tree near the cabin is nailed the list of seafood offerings: snapper, flounder, trout, salmon, shark, crabs, clams, frog's legs. The crabs go quickly, perhaps because they are dispatched using hammers, which motorcyclists have a fondness for. The table on which they were once heaped becomes, by early afternoon, an indescribably beautiful mess of glistening red shards. The meat is grilled on huge slabs of slatted iron or on chain-driven spits—pork, chicken, beef. A table with the requisite red-checked laminated plastic cloth offers paper plates and plastic utensils and, behind it, the requisite ladies ladling out portions of their homemade macaroni and potato salads.

A dispenser truck with taps in the side is parked among the trees. It gushes forth with the area's pride, Yuengling's beer, in light and dark varieties; the spigots are rarely off as lines of people take their turns placing plastic cups underneath. Birch beer arrives from a third tap, for those not inclined to drink and ride, and for the children flitting about underfoot. All the eating and talking is accompanied by a background noise of engines revving and cutting, for people are coming and going, and by the microphone being tested up on the flatbed of a truck on the lawn, so that after the bluegrass band plays some, Hermy can give away the door prizes. Since Herdan is also a BMW dealership—as well as a supplier of Triumph parts and, because even three brands of motorcycle can't make many shop owners a decent living, a purveyor of car tires—a lot of the prizes will bear the BMW stamp. There will be BMW key rings and tire tread gauges and coffee mugs and ear plugs (to provide relief from the whistling of the wind past a helmet, which can literally hurt). There will also be valuable leathers and winter gloves. Two years running the high point was a raffle for the last of the Excaliburs. In proof of the extraordinary range of people the picnic attracts, half of the crowd awaiting the pulling of the winning number from a basket by a little girl were cringing with dread while the other half clutched their ticket stubs in breathless hope. If you weren't thrilled to pieces to have one of these bikes for your own, it would be nearly impossible to find someone else outside of that afternoon's crowd to take it off your hands.

The band resumes its playing while a few couples dance arm in arm by the porch. Others sleep on their backs in the grass, having stayed up too late the night before trading the usual motorcycling war stories (the time one got caught in a blizzard in the western mountains and astonished the snowplow crews who thought they saw a strange phantom made of bad weather when a bike and rider came blithely by; the time another, after expressing sheer exuberance for a well-tuned engine, talked his way out of a ticket for doing 105 in a 45-mph zone). Some late arrivals on choppers pull up onto the lawn, and a woman in stunningly tight jeans overrevs the engine, slips the clutch, and slews the bike over sideways when the rear wheel spins so suddenly on the grass. People pretend not to notice too much, sensitive to the nature of humiliation. A fellow walks by wearing a T-shirt with a picture of the upstairs neighbor in *The Honeymooners*, and a lot of people get a good laugh at how twisting the context—from nonbike to bike—can turn a simple name like "Norton" into a witty gag.

SIX

*Three things are weakening: fear, sin, and travel.*
—*the Talmud*

I interviewed Robert MacNeil over the phone, went to PBS head-quarters for a batch of press releases, and sat down to the job my friend had phoned about before I left for New Hampshire with Franz: to produce a florid, idolatrous piece of hackwork on public television. I succeeded, and it ran as a color insert in the weekly magazine I had always wanted to appear in, though not in this way. Then I had the check—the one for five thousand dollars—that salves every hurt, and I began to muse over what to do with it. Windfalls, of course, must be spent immediately.

Actually, there was no contest. Riding was now a need, a creature that had to be fed. I asked Franz how much time he could take off from the shop, innocent of the fact that he could spare none, since the profit derived from owning a small motorcycle dealership was as substantial as vapor. He did not tell me he could not actually afford to leave for more than a day or two; he said that October might be passably slow, so he figured we could take a month. And then came

the suffusing pleasure of planning an itinerary, living with anticipation, the almost sexual delight of the zillion details that busy up pre-
trip life and begin to elevate it into the truly surreal. Franz brought
out his huge collection of maps, which included the old version of the
Blue Ridge Parkway guide, superior, Franz felt, to the new. He was
the authority on the Ridge, which he considered one of the greatest
motorcycling roads there was.

After that it was wide open. I consulted guidebooks, travel articles,
friends, and long-buried desires. I had never been to the Deep South,
although I had been romantically involved with the Civil War when
I was a girl. I also wanted to see the Paradise Garden constructed by
the Reverend Howard Finster in his Georgia backyard; Finster is an
"outsider" artist who had the call to build and paint and glue and mirror over stray bits of anything. Franz wanted to visit good friends in
Tallahassee, both artists, one a college teacher and bike freak as well.
Someone told me about a motel in Nashville with a pool shaped like
a guitar; I read about something called the "singing waters" of
Pascagoula. There was the Natchez Trace Parkway, and there was
food, for I longed to be in a place where every table sprouted bottles
of hot sauce and biscuits came with every meal. But it was New
Orleans that would be the point to which everything drew.

We got in shape by listening to Cajun music and arranging what
matters needed arranging before you disappear for a month. We
went to a big summer's-end Cajun festival on the piers in New York,
and when we saw that the food had been trucked up all the way from
Randol's Seafood & Restaurant in Lafayette, Louisiana, Franz and I
put that on our map too, sealing the pledge in the usual way.

It was high time for me to stop bungeeing duffel bags to the back
of my seat, so Franz helped me get outfitted right. At his recommendation, and dealer cost, I bought some soft saddlebags and a col-
lapsible tail sack. I got beautiful Italian leather gauntlet gloves with
studded palms. (I had already bought a real rainsuit.) And one Friday
Franz greeted me with not just his usual bouquet of flowers but also
with the demonstration of an electric vest that ran off the bike's bat-

tery. It sounded absurd to me, wimpy, yet when he said he wouldn't dream of traveling without his I bought that too.

FROM THE TRIP DIARY

DAY 1

In with a slam: trips don't so much start as ambush you. The anxiety of getting on the road, the denial that this is a *vacation*. And at the end: utter exhaustion, the need to detox.

Motels are strange halfway houses for half-lunatic travelers. What a cartload of stuff we two must lug in and out, in and out. A trip on bikes is a crash course in the wisdom of stripping down to next to nothing. And never does one feel so self-enclosed—a body moving through space, joining, touching, bouncing off whatever it comes across.

At night, a knife-sharp crescent moon, as if it had been plucked from the Turkish flag. Cold. No, I wouldn't sell my electric vest to anyone for any amount of dough, as Franz keeps taunting. Soon his offers will top twenty thousand dollars, and there I will sit, smug, shaking my head.

Suddenly, the South: the magazine rack at the Chevron carries hunting, gun, truck, fishing mags, and *Civil War Times Illustrated*. Gas-station convenience stores are the most elucidating museum display on a society's current concerns that you could imagine. Farther down I am sure we will see vast varieties of snuff start appearing on these shelves, although the need to make car interiors smell like the manufacturer's notion of strawberry, vanilla, and pine will no doubt remain constant.

DAY 2

Morning: Franz is out adjusting the valves on my bike. I have waked to the sight of the Blue Ridge Mountains outside the motel door, as if they arrived during the night. Coming in in the dark you are cushioned in your little envelope close about you—who knows

what is beyond? Every lit window looks magical and romantic. But
the daylight is a shower to wash off the night's lovely film. Then I
can more clearly dispose of my ridiculous wonderings of what life
would be like in this or that cozy valley, going to the night shift at
the furniture factory and coming home to a little family in a little
house—curious how in the night I forget that the shit follows you
around, no matter what life you try to take on.

Afternoon: One could never be prepared for the parkway, even if
one had dreamed of it for months. It must always appear unexpect-
edly, after an unsuspecting tour through a small town, up a little hill,
and a short turn: then you're *on* it. It has a quality of perennial anticipation about it. At first it seems in a state of preparedness to deliver
you to something else, as if it were a very long driveway to what
must be a marvelous chateau. That's probably because it doesn't
have the edges we expect from everything: curbs, signs, markers,
stay here, go there. Instead, its road surface melts into low-mown
grass; the rest is curves, curves, curves. And vistas, sometimes brilliant on both sides at once (of course, for this is a ridge)—overlooks
become quotidian, like gas stations and 7-Elevens on any other strip.
But you never get to the chateau, and then you realize: the drive is
it. Sweeping, it gives its rhythm to you, and you take on its life.

All the signs thus far have been more than auspicious (up to and
including the copy of the *I Ching* in our room tonight). After the
parking-lot fix-its this morning, I let my guide guide us, to Rowe's
Family Restaurant in Staunton, Virginia. A table full of blue-haired
ladies couldn't be all wrong, could they? Or the recommendation to
have the banana pudding?

But tonight was kept for real magic. Having reserved a room at
the Tuggles Gap Motel, we pulled up near frozen. (I was wearing
everything I had with me, including the priceless electric vest.) The
sight was dismaying. The parking lot was completely empty, and
seemed to have been so for generations. I half expected to hear the
soughing wind blowing the crisp leaves of ages past the decaying

motel in some sort of cinematic sound effect. So Franz ventured in (making no mention that we were the rare idiots who had actually called for a room) to ask if there was any other place to stay nearby. There was a place in Floyd, a few miles away, said a taciturn young man, but it's no good—why not stay here?

Since nothing could be no gooder than the Tuggles Gap Motel, we pressed on. My hands were agonizingly numb, and I knew that no matter how similarly depressing the rooms in Floyd, we wouldn't be going any farther.

If it were possible to avert your eyes while riding toward your goal, we would have done so. Instead we discovered the Pine Tavern and Lodge head-on. The tidy little room-cabins under the pines make you feel, Franz remarked, as if you're a guest in someone's home while he's away. One door down, at the tavern, you couldn't have ordered it up better from a fifty-item menu of what you'd give your eyeteeth to find at the end of a long, increasingly frigid road. Good and quite surprising food (of the seasoned-with-tamari-and-ginger kind; later we found out there had been more than one hippie commune around these parts, the only possible explanation for finding this sort of thing here). More unbelievable still was the quintet sitting around a large table playing Gaelic music. I ordered another glass of wine just so I could stay and listen while I wrote in this notebook. And here I sit, in the lap of serendipity.

DAY 3

Another glorious day. Buzzing airplanes—Quantico?

At one of those ubiquitous stunning overlooks, green mountains and valleys spread out into a blue-haze infinity, I lay back in the sunny grass and closed my eyes. Suddenly I heard a radio playing behind me. My annoyed thought: Who would disrupt the serenity of something like this with something like that? Then I said to myself, Lighten up, Pierson. Which was good, because I turned over to discover it was Franz's radio.

The speed limit on the parkway is forty-five. And you really wouldn't want to go more than that, except for those times when you want to go eighty-five or ninety. That's when the rhythm of the road *really* takes you.

DAY 4

This is a road built for nothing but pleasure, the pure pleasure of moving.

We ascended the great Mount Mitchell. And it's truly Mitchell's mount—there's something embarrassingly personal about it, as you discover by trekking up to the concrete observation tower, nosing touristically around, then realizing you're standing next to his lonely grave. He claimed this place not by trying to conquer it, but by trying to prove it was what it was: the highest elevation in the East. And you know it when you get there (your bike's power plant knows it before that; Franz laughed at the bottom of the ascent and said, "Want to hear what your bike sounds like with an old Japanese engine?"). The wind whips cold incessantly, and the Black Mountains around this one are too far down to be of any consequence.

Riding really takes it out of you. By seven we're cold, exhausted, famished. Tonight we made it to the Inn at Brevard, a typical country inn with pretentions, some fulfilled, others not. Certainly the bill is one of those amply fulfilled.

DAY 5

Almost too tired to think—a fitting end to the Blue Ridge, all 469 miles of it.

Got a pint of Rebel Yell (the ABC had over one hundred varieties of bourbon, surely a defining feature of heaven) and made another quick stop on the road through a gorge in the Great Smoky Mountains park for some boiled peanuts. They were useful mainly as a handwarmer. But I will never forget the sight of the cauldron sending up its mist into the darkness, or the half-insane little boy who danced around our bikes maniacally, or his father whiling away the time between customers watching the TV set outdoors under the pines, or the view of all of this vaporous scene growing more distant in my mirrors as we rode away into the blackness again, where I thought I heard a stream running next to us and sensed a high cliff, though it was probably my imagination.

In the middle of the night I woke up in this low-ceilinged Days Inn room, with a feeling that the darkness had been pressing interminably on my chest.

## DAY 6

This I could only be writing to the accompaniment of Rebel Yell.

Lookout Mountain in Chattanooga is the grand exemplar of a certain type of human ingenuity: a little natural beauty and some grasping entrepreneurship (the illustrious inventor of Tom Thumb miniature golf) meeting a surging need for "entertainment." And so they come in droves, to spend seven dollars a head for Ruby Falls—a lovely cave improved by some loud wisecracking guides, phony colored lights, and swelling music. The gift shops: nothing yet measures up to the grand junk emporia of Cherokee, North Carolina, with their embarrassment of plastic "gifts." In addition to the spare inner tube and spark plugs, I am now carrying around a set of cowboy and Indian figurines, a sheriff's badge pin, and a child's harmonica. I am not sure why.

Well, nothing will touch Paradise Garden—not at any time, maybe, but surely not at dusk. We asked in the local Pizza Hut how to find it, and the girls looked at one another: "Rev'rend Feenster?" Finally, "Oh, he-um! The crazy man!" His meticulously agglomerated monument will outlast most other things that pretend to matter. A hoodoo kingdom of painted wood, plastic beads, obsessiveness, in the midst of slumbering Summerville, Georgia.

We are taking State Route 27 right down the western Georgia

border, avoiding major highways, as is our custom. Today's rhetorical question: Which are there more of in these parts—Baptist
churches or those lighted mobile plastic signs with colored bulbs
around?

Tomorrow, we go to a Waffle House. Franz says they are to
breakfast what Cherokee is to cheap souvenirs—the kind of low-
down extravaganza I pine for, and so something to look forward
to....

DAY 7
The road follows the Chattahoochie River and provides a steady
increase in temperature, to the point of—now, at the Charter
House Inn in Bainbridge, Georgia, with its palm trees and Spanish
moss—near warm.

I had no idea there was this much space in Georgia. Or the kind
of town I thought had disappeared: old, broken-down, timeless,
every house in need of paint, the same dirty, wide-eyed kids and
scruffy dogs, no adults in sight.

Passing down the desolate, flat road, mile after mile of pines
flashing by, every couple of miles a sign for a hidden Baptist church
(but where are the people?), the monotony is broken only by a single reminder that the danger posed by the Georgia state patrol is
real—a lone black-and-white car secreted in the darkened corn-
fields on a patch of road that must see a car only every few hours
or so.

Thus far I have made every decision about where to go or what
to see. As soon as we land in a place, I look in the tourist pages of
the local phone book (my discovery is that they're a gold mine) to
see what hidden riches the area might hold. Franz agrees to everything. But he offers no ideas of his own. I am getting tired of being
the scout leader. I get testy and say, "Don't you have any interests
of your own?"

DAYS 8-10

We stayed with Franz's friends in Tallahassee, two talented artists who together make one hell of a couple. Their house is a jumble of folk art and baby toys. We took a short ride north into Havana, three of us with several feet to spare in the front seat of a sixties convertible Cadillac, under the pink-washed sky. We were going to Jim's enormous corrugated tin studio, the size of a warehouse, where he was constructing a monumental "wall of memories"— junk-store stuff hung on storm fencing—for an upcoming show. The building also housed scads of bikes: several Beemers, a lovely red Ducati, and a Suzuki GSX pocket rocket for his young son.

I laugh that it's October, we're stripped down and moving through moist air, and everything ahead of us is new. I can see the envy in Alexa's and Jim's eyes as we get ready to leave, although they have had their time—a month two-up on a bike with only a tankbag between them. "Go out and see it now," they say, "because it will soon be gone."

They have tipped us off to what our upcoming route west along the Gulf can offer, notably by way of food. And the happy-tacky resort of Destin, with the most beautiful beaches on the coast. Our off-season room with balcony in one of the high-rise hotels ringing the water was actually cheaper than many of the motels-as-necessities we've stayed at so far. We didn't want to leave its view for any longer than necessary and so rode to the grocery for smoked mozzarella, tomatoes, and bread, and ate our supper in the room with the lights off. The next day I swam from the powdered-sugar sand into emerald water as if I owned it. We just missed breakfast hour at the Silver Beach Hotel, the dining room of which defies description: toasters on every table, a statue of a "classical" nude out the window blocking the view of the Gulf.

DAY ?

I've lost count by now; New Orleans has intervened. We rode in on the threat of a hurricane making landfall near the city the next day. It was pouring all the way, but I felt hyped and happy—just another adventure to add to the list. How stupid. Franz had the presence of mind to remind me that wherever we found to stay, it would have to have indoor parking, or our bikes could end up flying out to sea.

We rode on out of the city through a storm that had been sent by the production designer of a sword-and-sandal epic—lashing, black. A few miles farther on the blue clawed through the screen, although my bike brought its memories with it: the mirrors, when I looked at them, were for miles twin tondos of chaos.

I got a new rear tire in New Orleans; it was Franz's idea before we left to send a tire ahead to that point on the map where he thought I would need it. It occurred to me, though I immediately let it go, that because I know he'll think about everything for me, I'll never bother to think about anything for myself. But isn't that what I want? A happy fantasy? After all, my bike is getting the best care in the world, making me feel like a mother whose kid is eating all its peas. And then the other little voice pipes up from below: Are you locked to Franz solely through the agency of your need to be taken care of? It made me suddenly feel a bit sick.

It is strange out in the bayous, where we spent a couple of days browsing—wide and flat, unreal cloud castles pitching far up into the sky, always the knowledge that water is out there somewhere. Then the enveloping dusk, and the sound like crickets or frogs. Hard liquor sales at gas stations. Fields of sugarcane. Fields of cows and horses. Expanses of goldenrod under the big sky. To satisfy the industrial aesthetic, oil wells and refineries like black skeletons in the distance. And every once in a while you come upon something you've read about, and it doesn't look anything like the pictures or the publicity. Sometimes I run across those only when I'm not look-ing for them, as when, bang, turning in to the tourist info center at Opelousas I ended up parking right in front of the "Jim Bowie Museum"—a ramshackle one-room cabin—that I'd read about but

*The motorcycle passenger sometimes takes the position of third wheel. In 1906 Mr. and Mrs. Willie Kay took the air on their Indian Tricar. (Prints & Photographs Division, Library of Congress)*

*Women riders have long attracted both stigma and benefit as a result of being highly noticeable. Early in the century, Clara Wagner's fame as an endurance racer was capital to the Eclipse Machine Company, as shown by this advertising postcard. It bears a note on back claiming that "Miss Clara Wagner the most successful and experienced lady motorcyclist always uses the Eclipse Coaster Brake." Her renown also contributed to a rash of rather aggressive insecurity among race organizers.*

*A very happy man: "Weishaar, winner of 100 mi. race. Norton, Kan. Oct. 22 '14. Time 2 hr. 1½ min. World Record."  It probably stood, too, at least until the following afternoon. (Prints & Photographs Division, Library of Congress)*

*Taking the scenic route in a 1933 race, probably in California. (Prints & Photographs Division, Library of Congress)*

War, in general a perfectly tautological enterprise, used motorcycles to gun men down and then to carry away those hit (in particular, as in the two pictures below, Indians on behalf of American troops in World War I; British units similarly employed Royal Enfields as machine-gun mounts). By World War II, the motorcycle dispatch rider was a romantic figure, a "motorized cowboy," as in this Belgian boys' story.

Let it not be said that motorcycles have no socially redeeming use. In the instructional photo at left, illustrating a 1922 edict that was to make Washington, D.C., cops "politest in nation" (courteous tone of voice, no "bawling out"), a fast woman gets a ticket for 25 in an 18 zone. *(Prints & Photographs Division, Library of Congress)*

Below, *the potentials of commerce are improved by Harley-Davidson's Servi-Car, introduced in 1931 as an efficient means to tow disabled automobiles to a garage.* *(Courtesy Ronald G. Hand)*

*The running start of the 350cc event in the 1951 Dutch TT. Number 53, at center, is a Norton (with famed "featherbed" frame) piloted by Geoffrey Duke, who would take World Championship laurels for the year in both 350 and 500cc classes. (Photo John Schaepman)*

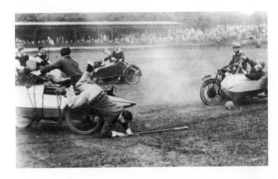

*There Will Always Be an England: A vigorous game of sidecar polo at the King's Oak track, Loughton, date unknown. Britons have even been known to use sidecars in cross-country scrambles, where they frequently become airborne. (Prints & Photographs Division, Library of Congress)*

*"Mike the Bike" Hailwood in form on a 500cc MV Agusta in 1963, the year he won the World Championship. Ditto in 1962, 1964, and 1965; on 250s in 1961, 1966, and 1967; and on 350s in 1966 and 1967. He had a stirring comeback win at the Isle of Man in 1978 at the age of 38 aboard a 900cc Ducati, and the company quickly trotted out a production "Hailwood Replica" model. (Photo J. L. Ranscombe)*

*Grandmothers are bikers, too, as this undated photo of a chipper Clara B. Brown of Leamington, England, attests. Its original caption maintains that she "has achieved a feat without parallel by learning to ride a motorcycle when over 50 years of age. She daringly makes frequent lone spins and spends her holidays in extended tours of the whole country, while she is recognized by the clubs as being their oldest lady member." (Prints & Photographs Division, Library of Congress)*

*In 1941 in Essex Junction, Vermont, a carnival barker attracts an audience for motorcycle daredevils, who from the beginning of the century were as often as not women. Nothing could be more exciting than watching them challenge gravity on the Wall of Death, a wooden cylinder with 20-foot-high walls that was perhaps evolved from banked board tracks. An American troupe of Wall of Death riders — including one "Plucky Jennie Perry" — toured the world in 1929, and a newspaper reported of their South African performance, "No wonder we cheered with relief when these intrepid motor cyclists once more reached terra firma." (Photo Jack Delano, Farm Security Administration collection, Prints & Photographs Division, Library of Congress)*

*Though largely a secret from the general public, most motorcyclists have at one time or another ridden down the highway singing at the top of their lungs. Doing so more tunefully than most is Elvis, in 1964's* Roustabout.

You meet the nicest people on a Honda

HONDA

The sixties saw the tide turn once more in favor of motorcycling as acceptable activity for "nice" people; Honda targeted the youth market, bringing them into showrooms in droves (this one photographed in 1966 by Warren K. Leffler for U.S. News & World Report). *(Prints & Photographs Division, Library of Congress)*

*Something about being in a group of motorcyclists just makes you want to line up and get on film. Note the natty suits in the first photo, possibly from the teens or twenties (Courtesy Ronald G. Hand); the more casual look sported by the San Antonio Dragons in 1941; and the early twentieth-century rotating panoramic camera ready to take in the crowd at a recent Moto Guzzi rally in West Virginia.*

*According to the message on back of this Harley-Davidson advertising card, Richard E. New nearly met his maker on June 26, 1912, when his parachute failed to open at 1700 feet. "An awning broke his fall," his legs were amputated at the knees, and thus he had to use some ingenuity when it came to riding a bike. His modern counterpart is Bob Nevola, who modifies his machines so he can ride without the use of a left arm. Nevola is the founder of the National Handicap Motorcyclist Association, a clearinghouse of information for disabled bikers. (Courtesy Bob Nevola)*

*The V50 tries going glamour queen at a photographer's studio, where she was admired but never made it to print.*

*Franz gets a shot of our two bikes on the Blue Ridge. Less than a year later I return alone, posing for a stranger at the same spot. Probably the only smile of that trip.*

*John Leffler demonstrates correct road repair procedure: Hand over credit card; load bike into U-haul; drive to where you can get parts; fit new electronic ignition. Later, John helps me identify by ear the point at which the throttle slide has opened in the Lario's left carb.* (Photo Bob Sweeny)

*Readying our machines for the first all-women CLASS riding course at New Hampshire International Speedway in 1995.*

*Luc Van Vossel eats up the miles on his Moto Guzzi Le Mans 1000; David Smith in a rare moment off a bike.*

*An extremely trick, heavily modified Guzzi at a rally in Germany; the gas tank is lightweight aluminum and the motor is a good fifteen years old but tweaked into the nineties. According to one commentator, Moto Guzzi is "the Lancia of the motorcycle world, as the Italian car firm is famous for doing everything in a different way from everyone else and favoring complexity for its own sake."*

*The Motorradmuseum Otterbach displays motorcycles with proper reverence.*

decided not to look for, because I'd never find it. Shadows-on-the-Teche was another of those places I forgot about looking for, therefore located, and since the plantation house was a property of the National Historic Trust and I am my father's child, I had to stop.

When we arrived in Lafayette I started to phone Randol's to make a dinner reservation, whereupon Franz leaned back on the bed and said he wasn't going. I beg your pardon? We'd come seventeen hundred miles for this date, and now he didn't feel like it? What really steamed me was that he lay silent, walled off, his eyes cold and resolute. I got back on the bike and tore to the restaurant, where I had an expensive meal by myself and watched the couples whirling in the *salle à danser.* I didn't have a very good time, but I didn't reckon I'd have had one back in the motel room, either.

Today, temperatures in the thirties, and the Natchez Trace Parkway. Its charms are subtler than those of the Blue Ridge, and in the cold it feels like ours, all its sweeping length; top gear to the end. An eerie wind seemed to be blowing by my cheek from the past as I stood down in one of the deep depressions that marks a portion of the original trace—I was communing with those who had also walked there but disappeared, my feet in the footprints of the dead.

There the trip diary ends. By the time we got back, we had covered five thousand miles.

But the gravest problem is that I don't lose my nerve before I jump. Hell, I don't feel I have a problem. I have a situation. I don't have any problems in life, just situations. I'm positive I can jump the Grand Canyon because I'm a firm believer in the fact that any idea that a man can honestly conceive and honestly believe, if he wants to do the thing really bad enough, he can do it.

I don't care if they say, "Look, kid, you're going to drive that thing off the edge of the Canyon and die," I'm going to do it. I want to be the first.

. . . I want to do something that's never been done before. . . . I believe we were born dead. I did not ask to be put here on earth. I have accepted that dying is a part of living. . . . I want to do this thing because I want to do this thing. I don't know if it's going to make a worthwhile contribution to society or transportation, but I'm going to do it.

—Evel Knievel, quoted in "He's Not a Bird, He's Not a Plane," *Sports Illustrated*, February 5, 1968

Over the century, motorcycles have joined single-engine airplanes and one-person sailboats as among the premier tools by which human focus and endurance can be tested. The urge to go on unprecedentedly long, lonely trips or to do something that has never been done before is another one that is persistent past all reason. Some people may simply be wired differently. In July 1991, Gerard d'Aboville started out rowing solo across the Pacific; he had already rowed across the Atlantic in seventy-two days. Said his wife, Cornelia, "I've been asked, 'Why, why, why?' And I don't know why."

That is a fitting epigraph to most of the attempts to venture into untraveled territory via car, glider, motorcycle, or any similarly simple conveyance. The teens and the twenties were an especially ripe time for this sort of journey; the papers were filled with excited announcements of so-and-so setting off across continents or seas, waved away by crowds of well-wishers. This season of daring treks included the Great Air Race of 1924, in which a group of men flew a Liberty-engined Douglas open-cockpit plane around the world. They met Aloha Baker, driving a car around the world in the other direction, in Calcutta, the halfway point for both.

The earliest circumnavigation of the globe by bike is probably that of American Carl Stevens Clancy, who reportedly piloted a Henderson Four eighteen thousand miles in 1912. Further information is hard to come by.

Much better documented, for they wrote a book about it, is the trip made by the Frenchmen Robert Sexé and Henry Andrieux. Riding two 350cc, 3½-hp Gillet Sport models (made in Liège, Belgium), they departed Paris in June 1926. Their itinerary took them through Moscow, Yokohama, San Francisco, New York, London, and back to Paris in early December of the same year— 25,000 kilometers. The Sport was thereafter dubbed the Tour du Monde, and an example of one is now displayed in a crypt in the former abbey in Stavelot, Belgium, that houses the motor museum of the Spa-Francorchamps raceway.

Nothing poses starker evidence of the fact that the world has changed in the past sixty years than the books written by round-the-world motorcyclists in the thirties. (Nothing, that is, except possibly the film footage taken by at least two of these authors.) The dangers of going over Niagara Falls in a barrel remain fairly constant over the generations, but roads, lodgings, and border patrols will never be as unforgiving as they were then.

*Going Further*, published in 1931, is the account of the 22,800 miles traversed by two Britons in sidecar rigs. Or it purports to be; it could be more accurately described as the author's extended complaint against prevailing bad roads and natives who did not sufficiently jump to in providing cool drinks in the desert when they were requested; what we see of the way things were is largely past his shoulder when he chances to move from the center of the scene.

The author is Geoffrey Malins, and he does not deign to identify himself, his exact date of departure, or even his much-praised motorcycles; we know only that he was accompanied by a man named Charles Oliver, they left London most probably in 1929, and the machines were 1000cc British-built twins (nicknamed Pip and Squeak). We can surmise from hints in the text that he was a captain in the RAF—Britain's reach was such that there were few continents, and especially oases thereon, that did not offer ample opportunity for a worthy to don evening clothes to share drinks with his cronies at the officers' club—and the record of their trip is often one of lackeys scurrying ahead with supplies and remote outposts rallying warm welcomes at the presentation of a letter of introduction from some colonial governor or commander-in-chief.

Not that they could avoid adventures entirely; most resulted in busted springs and axles, though the relative simplicity of their machinery meant they could fairly quickly improvise the kind of fixes—and every other day on the vicious terrain seemed to require one or more—that today's vehicles would not allow. The sands of Arabia in particular hid devilish surprises. Riding into a village one night when he felt compelled to make more tracks, Malins was nagged into stopping by a sixth sense that kept telling him something was wrong. He assumed it was his motorbike, even though it seemed to be running perfectly. Continuing on the next day, in the light, he soon came upon the source of his premonition: a missing bridge over a deep wadi, a dry streambed, which in the darkness would have surely swallowed up his rig and possibly put an end to his trip.

A few years later an American would also write in a book about an eerily similar circumstance, only he managed to fall through the nonexistent span of bridge into the wadi—fifteen feet down, as night was coming on. As he lay unconscious in the Turkish sand, his prone motorcycle dispatched its oil into the ground. Although he was quickly rescued by nearby villagers—whom he describes with a generosity of detail completely absent from Malins's document—he was still fifty miles from the nearest supplies. The only thing he could do was try to convey to the natives what it was he lacked, and hope they could provide it. The closest they could come was thick yellow mustard oil. On attempt, it seemed to work. The rider started away, only to realize, at the sight of the exhaust he left behind, that he was producing true mustard gas in clouds.

The American, Robert Edison Fulton, Jr., was scarcely less well-born than Geoffrey Malins. His father was the president of the Mack Truck Company, and young Fulton attended Harvard and then studied architecture in Vienna. At the conclusion of that year he found himself at a London dinner party, where he surprised both himself and the other guests by announcing that he intended to ride around the world on a motorcycle. From the end of the table came a voice: "If you haven't your motor yet, old man, then how about letting me furnish it? You know, we have the Douglas motor works. Fine engines. We must talk this over."

Thus he received his Douglas, a 750-pound, 6-hp horizontally opposed twin on which he would ride forty thousand miles of paved road, desert sand, and mountain gravel, and even, after the Khyber Pass with the Afghan frontier in sight, twenty yards with roles of machine and man reversed, the bike laboriously crab-walked by its owner because of regulations that forbade riding motorcycles in the Khyber District.

*One Man Caravan* is a delicious book—visually, for its artistically adept author filled it with handsome maps, woodcuts, and stills from the film footage he took all along his way; and as an entertaining, well-written portrait of a disappeared world, from the pen of an enthusiastic twenty-two-year-old who had a nearly bottomless capacity for enjoying things.

Nor was (or is) long-distance trekking an exclusively male affair. The *New York Times* reported in 1913 that a Mrs. Harry Humphreys ("champion long-distance rider of England") had finished the San Francisco–to–New York leg of a projected 85,000-mile trip. I can find no record of what might have happened to her on such a mythically proportioned journey, how long she might have lasted into the two years it was supposed to take, or whether she received the ten-thousand-dollar prize she was to pocket if she made it back to California in time for the 1915 opening of the Panama Pacific Exposition.

Brooklynite Effie Hotchkiss decided to take her mother to the same San Francisco exposition—intended to be a grand celebration of the latest advances in science and industry, and an obvious destination for those who believed motorcycles would be in every vanguard of the promised new world—in her Harley sidecar rig; their successful round trip took five months and nine thousand miles. More widely celebrated was the 1916 transcontinental record set by sisters Adeline and Augusta Van Buren, the first women to ride solo motorcycles across the country, as well as the first to climb Pikes Peak in any type of vehicle. In 1953, Peggy Iris Thomas published *Gasoline Gypsy,* telling of her experiences after leaving London in 1950 with a BSA Bantam, sixty dollars, and the intention to see North America. "A girl riding a motorcycle loaded like a pack mule with suitcases and camping equipment causes enough stir. However, if she is accompanied by a sixty-pound Airedale dog as well, things tend to get out of hand," Thomas modestly wrote.

People continue to make epic journeys on two wheels because, like Fulton, they want a way to feel fully engaged with and even vulnerable to their surroundings. Many people feel free to come up and talk when you are on a bike; you have eschewed certain protections and shields in exchange for the fullest possible experience of a place. And there is the appealing athleticism of the endeavor—on a long trip across continents, you will get bruised, baked, and knocked about, and be given plenty of opportunities to challenge your physical and technical wits. The resulting rugged experience has the effect of reordering one's priorities, making one look at the scope of a single life a little differently. It has much in common with camping (and indeed is often combined with camping) and with what camping can teach. Motorcycle journeyers would no doubt sense an echo of the familiar in what John Burroughs wrote early in this century in "A Summer Voyage": "The camper-out often finds himself in what seems a distressing predicament to people seated in their snug, well-ordered houses; but there is often a real satisfaction when things come to their worst,—a satisfaction in seeing what a small matter it is, after all; that one is really neither sugar nor salt, to be afraid of the wet; and that life is just as well worth living beneath a scow or a dugout as beneath the highest and broadest roof in Christendom."

One trip undertaken for that satisfaction, and for its own rambling, extraordinary sake, though it may well have entered the record books because of the ardor with which its extensiveness was pursued, is that of Briton Ted Simon, who took four years to travel 63,000 miles through forty-five countries. He is also a writer, which shows in *Jupiter's Travels*, the 1979 book about his incredible journey, comprising (of course) both the internal and external ones.

You may have to take my word for the fact that traveling by bike is superior to traveling by car. All right—I will allow that it's very, very different. Especially in the dark: the road seems to tilt ever upward, and you start imagining things. There will be rivers rushing in the blackness near the roadside; there will be a cliff looming overhead. You can ride into imaginative space, which is *real* traveling, because you are not anchored by anything. Look around. There is nothing between you and the weather, the smells, the color of the sky. All impress themselves on your consciousness as if the ride had turned it to wet cement. And there they will stay, apparently forever, so you can recall those sensations with an almost frightening precision years later.

The cold may get down in your bones—and in the case of Franz, it will get deep inside the steel rods that you can feel, hard and confounding, under the flesh of one thigh; this was the result of an accident that occurred when he was taking a customer's bike for a shakedown ride and the reason for his squatting on the chair behind the shop counter. It was also the cause of some excruciating backaches. Anyway, the cold may get in your bones and down your neck, but I think you will almost enjoy it: a little penance for all the prizes.

For some reason, riding the interstates on a motorcycle confers automatic, if only temporary, membership in the brotherhood of truckers. Often in a car I've felt I was the sixteen-wheeler's enemy, annoyingly in the way of a proper eighty-five on a downgrade and chugging forty on the incline. But on a bike I've felt protected by trucks, given wide berth, leeway to pass, signals on the all-clear. Maybe it's because so many drivers are bikers too. Maybe it's because both vehicles become more like comrades than agglomerations of parts. Or maybe it's because everyone needs friends out there in the big bad world.

I love truck stops, even though I've grown to hate writers' waxing poetic about them; they're too obvious. They are beacons of home light in the dark anonymity of the multilane, making us wish for an inner glimpse of those multitudinous lives that go on without us but might hold some clue to understanding our own. These men with their cowboy boots and straw hats and big belt buckles, black Harley eagle T-shirts and Cat caps and big guts—so easy to endow them with a downside spirituality that might become transparent and available if we just hung around these mysterious waysides variously offering family-size bags of cookies, guns, air fresheners with girlie pictures, and stick-on plastic mugs with no-spill lids. If we can just read and understand the songs on the jukebox selectors on the counter in front of us, Merle and Hank Jr. and Tammy and, hand-printed, a bunch of truckers' tunes. If we can divine the rituals of showers and flirtations with waitresses and the inexplicable girls with big hair and the CB talk and just what it is they think about up there in the cabs for hours and hours on end. But maybe it's no mystery at all; maybe it's just a job.

One of the great appeals of traveling by bike, in contrast to trucks, is the necessity of relying on what you can fit in the bags, and the discovery that you can do more with less. As Peter Matthiessen noted to an interviewer about a similar activity, it provides an existential relief: "One reason I like boats so much is that you have to pare everything down to the bare necessities, and there you are, the captain of a little boat, without a shelter, without a past, without future hopes."

Maybe it was when we all settled down those eons ago, gave up our wandering ways and abandoned hunting and gathering—traveling light because always traveling—that things got truly messed up. Now we strive to collect, bury ourselves under heaps of things, and, so burdened, can no longer hear the whisper of the land summoning us out onto it. That's what Bruce Chatwin thought, and so much of what he wrote was by way of formulating a proof that the walls of our houses are the walls between us and our true calling—to move ceaselessly over the earth, according to its directives.

If we had remained mobile, like the aborigines, we too might have retained eyes like theirs, capable of seeing the natural world. As Chatwin described it in *The Songlines*, the aborigines' "religious life had a single aim: to keep the land the way it was and should be." Our aim, in our fixed world with eyes turned ever inward, is just as single-minded, it seems: to accumulate goods. At the end of this metaphoric road stands the nonmetaphoric Kmart, glistening like Oz and filled to the rafters with a hundred cheap mementos of wildflowers, in forms of candle, air freshener, sachet, cologne, bath bead, potpourri, and incense stick. In its prior life, of course, the ground under the big store bloomed with wildflowers.

Is this too obvious an irony? Is it too late? I sway between hope and despair. At the moment, even the growing movement based on simplifying life has spawned more commodities, books and magazines that tell you how to get there. But one uninstructed option remains to pack a very small bag and hit the road.

When you go alone, if you are like me, you remain alone. It is so easy to strike up friendships when you're on a bike it should overcome even my pathological shyness, but alas that is not always the case. So I get a lot of thinking done; I have composed great poems at sixty miles an hour, but there they stay, hovering over the macadam, reluctant to be brought home.

When you go with someone else, you are in for either the ride of your life or a series of greater or lesser annoyances. Riding together is like dancing, and when you are hearing the same music and the same beat in your blood, you can communicate without words, anticipate every stop, start, fluctuation of desire, speedup and slowdown. When you are not, your partner keeps knocking your knee with his until you can't hear the music anymore, and even your motorcycles seem mismatched, with the one in the lead invariably digging in at a cruising speed that is exactly the one at which the bike behind aches to change gear. You might as well ride alone in that case and stop for lunch when you want to.

If all the country-western songs ever written were compressed into one (and a hell of a song it would be, too, with Hank Williams, Roy Acuff, and the Carter Family singing at once), the gist of the lyrics would be something like this: *Get out of my way, honey, 'cause a roaming man's just got to roam; but when I'm out there roaming I feel like hell 'cause I miss the green hills of home so much I could cry.*

Paradox no longer makes me shiver, not since I started riding away from home in order to feel the sweet sensation of missing it at the same time I love leaving it.

The only motorcycle magazine I ultimately keep a subscription to, after flirting with all the others, is *Rider.* This is not necessarily a testament to its excellence—it is more than a tad amateurish, although it has some good writers—but rather to the repetitive dullness of the others. Their predominantly young male staffs, headquartered near California's best canyon-racing roads, have a good thing going and they know it: all the free whiz-bang machinery they can handle. So they endlessly test the latest crotch rockets and occasionally throw in a comparison of the new cruisers or a thrilling piece inevitably titled "Oil for Your Bike: Fact and Friction." (Actually, I just made that up.) But *Rider,* while several constellations distant from the quality of even the least of British bike publications, at least tries.

Thus one month it had a column, by an *éminence grise* named Clement Salvadori, about motorcycling books. That library shelf is relatively short. But Salvadori had unearthed some interesting titles, and I sent off a friend who had a membership at New York's

Mercantile Library to see if he could locate any of the older books I had failed to find in the New York Public Library. He came back with Robert Edison Fulton, Jr.'s *One Man Caravan*.

How I hated to let that beautiful book go back to the library.

One month later I was snuffling through a secondhand book barn in Pennsylvania. I always go to the automotive or transportation shelves first, just to satisfy myself that there aren't any bike books growing mildew there; there rarely are. At best there are a few shop manuals and one or two of the illustrated encyclopedias I already have. But this time it was different. They had one book, and it was one I did not yet own.

*One Man Caravan*, 1937. With a dust jacket. First edition. The author's signature on the flyleaf.

I was feeling poor that day, and I decided the twenty-dollar asking price was too rich for my blood. I carried it around the barn for two hours, then told the friend I was with I was going to put it back. He looked at me like the feebleminded wretch I was and took it from my hands and wordlessly marched to the cashier.

On the way home I started doing math in my head. If Fulton was twenty-two in the early thirties, how old would he be now? Well, old. But it was just possible that he was living in the New York area.

I called the publisher of the book, Harcourt Brace. It had on file addresses for the author current to the fifties, the last of which was care of an airline at an airfield in Connecticut. I sent a letter off into space, fairly certain it would land in the modern equivalent of the dead-letter office, and forgot about it.

But I can never forget, a month later, the evening before New Year's Eve. It was powerfully cold outside, which meant you could feel the frigid air with your hand an inch away from my apartment's thin walls; in the winter I became like a heat-seeking cat, spending much of my time standing next to the special old gas stove in the kitchen that provided the apartment's only warmth. I was pressed up against its vents, staring absently toward the windows I had ringed with little white Christmas lights, when the phone rang. The voice on the other end was strong and clear, and it said, "This is Robert Fulton."

He invited me to visit him at his farm in Connecticut; he would pick me up at the train station. We spent the afternoon, which felt dreamlike and dislocated to me, sitting in the art studio appended to the converted barn he and his French-born wife lived in; outside the floor-to-ceiling window was snow-swept lawn on which was parked the World War II P-51 Mustang fighter plane that had superseded his bike. He showed me his photo collages, the sculptures and fountains he had devised and set about the property, the inventions and scrapbooks that described his life since returning from his long journey by motorcycle. He was indeed a descendant of his namesake, Robert Fulton, steamboat inventor, and among his eclectic brainchildren was a device that enabled World War II tailgunners to target-practice while on the ground without wasting ammunition; the Airphibian, a small plane that could be converted to an automobile in five minutes by one person (an example is in the Smithsonian's collection); and, most famously, Skyhook, a unique method whereby a person on the ground can be rescued by a specially equipped but otherwise standard airplane flying overhead, which never has to land to accomplish its mission. The U.S. military has a lock on the use of this ingenious contrivance.

Fulton is, really, as handsome now as he was in the stills in his book (the film is yet unedited, but he has at last begun splicing). He flits about from project to project, his mind solving problems almost without conscious intervention and his hands fashioning the prototypes that prove it. He writes and sculpts and draws, only he does not just write a book now, he also creates a new method of typesetting to print it.

A couple of years ago his stepson and a friend set off from Paris on new motorcycles, intending to re-create Fulton's great ride around the world. They became separated some time into the trip, and his wife's son was killed on the road, not halfway around.

In December I persuaded Franz to throw a party in his loft, the first
he'd ever had, where we served red beans and rice, as we'd eaten at
the Sunday-night fais-do-do at Tipitina's in New Orleans, and invited the guests to show slides from their favorite bike trips. I was so
nervous about trying to engineer the right effect that I neglected to
eat although not to drink, and ended the evening throwing up into
the bathtub, still in my party dress, the first time since freshman year
of high school that I had so forgotten myself.

But Franz was not really the entertaining type, nor was he going
to get a lift for his shoe as I kept nagging him to, which would even
out his legs and prevent the debilitating backaches, not to mention
the deformation of his foot. He was not likely to transform himself
into another sort of person, either, the kind I kept hoping he would
become: one who loved books or understood what they could mean
to a person. And I had discovered he had a secret, one that he was not
so much hiding from me as from himself. I began to think of him as
a mountain I felt too tired to climb. One day he hurled a glass ashtray into the sink from across the room with such sudden force at
something I said that I picked up my bags to leave without saying
another word. A month or two before, he had stopped greeting me
every weekend with flowers.

The only thing of mine he still has is a set of hand-painted
Provençal dishes I had bought at a thrift shop somewhere out the
Main Line. A couple of years later, when we were talking again, I
came to the shop on an errand and asked him if I could run over to
the loft to pick them up. He lent me the key, which I'd always had
trouble with. But this time, no matter what I did, I could not open
that door. I stood outside trying to work the lock for fifteen minutes
before giving up. He told me one of the plates had broken, anyway.

That May I decided to go down the Blue Ridge again. Part of the reason, although I certainly was not admitting it to myself, was that I
knew Franz was planning his annual jaunt down there with his bud-
dies. Even though I recognized I was right to have instigated the

split, I wanted him to want me back anyway, and to want to ride with me instead of them, even if I also knew I would refuse him. I wanted him to feel as lonely as I was.

## FROM THE TRIP DIARY

### MAY 9

It was a long ride in the rain. And the wind. And then the sun, then more rain. I stood in the entryway of a 76 Auto/Truck stop, watching the rain sheeting across the parking lot and over my bike. I discovered a leak in the rear drive, but there was nothing to do about it at this point except wipe it off and see if it reappeared.

The truckers coming and going through the double doors made their comments—"It looks like rain," said one clever fellow—in their thick yuckabilly accents. Another guy seemed about two inches from the edge. As he passed me struggling to put my rain gear back on, he let out a howl that was like nails on a blackboard, crying to the ceiling, "Let it rain, oh, let it rain!"

Creep.

But then the sun came out. And a wide-open highway, and the West Virginia spring all around. Suddenly a scent of it—more inscrutable than just things growing—and a sob came up in my throat.

### MAY 10

Fifty miles after I first wiped it off, there was an equally copious amount of 90-weight all over the drive housing. So I called Franz from the parking lot of the Southern Kitchen restaurant, where I'd just had a cup of peanut soup.

Maybe it was the breather cap, gummed up with junk from the rain and now backing things up, forcing oil through the seal of the nut. He told me to take it off, clean it, and blow through it to make sure it was clear. He laughed when he told me he would be thinking of me standing there with that metal cap between my lips, gently blowing. I felt it was cruel to flirt with me if he was going to persist in being three hundred miles away.

I'm less than twenty miles from Floyd now, my destination for the

night. So I've stopped at an overlook, which at first looked as if it
might be the same one we stopped at for a rest in October. But no,
it's not. What am I doing anyway, looking to re-create that trip,
when it's foreordained to hurt me now?

Here, at Smart View (the brochure says there was a cabin here, of
which it was said it had "a right smart view"), the colors are that
supersaturated type found in postcards from the sixties. Only it's the
way things really look.

The scale of things on the road is sometimes intimate, sometimes
so big it makes you scared. Sometimes you're in flat country, but it's
way up in the air. And sometimes it makes you feel lonely, like here,
with the wind in the high tops of the trees and the constant crickets, hidden, and the distant thunder of planes in the air.

No, you should never try to go back. What a dumbass idea to get
an assignment to write about Floyd. As soon as I arrived it seemed
just moments ago that we had been here together. She gave me the
same room we'd had.

MAY 14

There is a sweet scent in the air, although I can't seem to find
where it comes from; I can't see any likely flower among the young
green. Virginia is achingly beautiful. And it's sunny, although it is a
bit "airish," as someone in the Deep South remarked to us on a
cool day last fall.

I will know better in the future to plan some destination for the end
of the trip, instead of the return home trailing off like a pointless
sentence. With no real reason for dragging it out, for spending
many more nights locked alone into motel rooms with takeout food
and my own bad company, I suddenly grabbed at the map to see if I
could go all the way home in a single day. But no matter what route
I chose, or how long I figured I could ride without dropping, there
was no way to do it. I will have at least two more nights on the
road. It seems so long I could cry.

# SEVEN

*The cobbles had long since been replaced by a layer of asphalt, and she was not naive to the point of being unaware that it was a machine she was riding, and that a motor, even one as powerful as the Harley-Davidson's, had no impulsion of its own, but when she fed it gas and it leaped forward, it was with so much intoxication that she let herself be carried away that the motorcycle always seemed to her the last scion of the great funereal horses of the past centuries. . . .*
—*André Pieyre de Mandiargues*, The Motorcycle

It was well over ninety stifling degrees when I hit the glorious New York Thruway. Going into the nose, the air felt like smoke from a brushfire. For a moment the surface of the parking lot at the first service plaza I stopped at seemed made of that black rubber matting they put under swingsets in public playgrounds, but no, it was simply the ground melting. I had been riding the poor Lario hard, and in my mind I apologized to her and her air-cooled cylinders, which could not have been cooled much by this air. She was a noble horse who suffered much. But today it was in the interest of relief, for I was going north, north. My imagination had it that every mile farther north we got, the temperature would decline a fraction.

Our destination—and I most often needed a destination in order to get on the bike, because I didn't see much point in simply going for a circular ride—was another rally. It was in Parry Sound, Ontario, north even of Toronto, which sounded nice and wintry. I was, as usual, hurrying to get there, even though I had given myself an ample two days to do it.

I was encouraged to slow down only when I reached the Adirondacks, whose trees and altitudes and gentle warmth made riding the perfect pleasure. I stopped for a root beer, from a brown bottle embossed with cowboys, and an ice cream cone, the kind of treats-from-the-past that are most appropriate to the area. I was growing about as relaxed as I ever got while traveling by myself, when usually I had to force myself to make a stop, even though my bladder had long been screeching for help or my stomach protesting its needs in minor sea squalls, and even then I would only pause long enough to get take-out sandwiches to eat in a few gulps outside on the curb where I could be eye level with the Lario's carburetors. On other occasions, riding with my dear friend John (him of the garage full of bikes, and the eloquence to term them charismatic objects) for any length of time was something of a trial for me. In direct contrast to mine, his manner is best described with the word *deliberate*. The admirable intensity he brings to a mechanical challenge—first aligning it with the celestial map of the cosmos he carries in his head while regarding it at a reasonable distance down his nose through reading glasses, murmuring to himself as he approaches, then turning things experimentally this way and that—is problematic when applied to the menu at a highway Big Boy. Usually I've shredded my napkin under the table, and shredded the shreds, by the time John leans back ("Aaah," he says) and announces his intention to enjoy a second cup. He proceeds to drink it while making small sounds of satisfaction to himself. "Mmmm, mmmm . . ." he says. It is rarely what I am feeling.

I don't know if it's white-line fever that makes me ride like this or if it's due to what Uncle George used to mean when I was a kid and he told me I had ants in my pants. Actually, I think I do know the answer.

The plan was to venture through the unknown-to-me western reaches of the huge Adirondack Park via Route 3, past Fort Drum, into and out of Watertown, and on to Cape Vincent, where I would await the ferry to Wolfe Island and Canada. As a violently painted dusk winched itself down over the landscape, I kept riding. I passed Lake Placid, Saranac Lake, Tupper Lake. On their shores I could see motels and guest cabins shaded by pines, enjoying a lightly scented breeze; people were splashing in the water on this warm July evening. I would have loved a swim to wash off the thin crust of salt that crumbed my skin. I would have benefited from sitting back on a porch and sitting still. I kept riding. Wonderful lodging possibilities presented themselves in succession, and each time I said: Just a little farther; a little farther and there might be something even better.

A little farther, the land flattened out. The trees were gone. The guest cabins had fled. The few cars I passed looked rusted and big and old and rode skewed and low as though their owners were getting the last few miles out of them before the struts collapsed completely. Evening deepened until night covered us. I now hoped I would see another motel, period, much less one with a lake view. Besides, it was starting to rain.

At last. I didn't dare hope it would be the more favorable of the two types of motel: the one whose rooms are pure haven, a warm, gently glowing nest, a home away from home that is far better than home because it is a fantasy home offering only comfort. Opening the door onto the other kind, however, you can hear a dim splash echo, the sound of something landing deep in the abandoned well of the soul. These rooms have a hollow, disused-rec-room air about them, and as soon as you enter your skin feels coated with despair.

That was what it was like at the Bartlett Pair Motel, and I noticed there was nary another guest partaking of its charms. No one but me to enjoy its mildewed bedcovers, the room's one cardboard "painting" nailed up on its Masonite walls. This was the *No Exit* of overnight accommodations.

At about three in the morning the lightning made like the sun, turning the grayed polyester drapes luminescent white. The thunder boomed, shaking the world, like an underground detonation. It was not possible for there to be any more rain falling from the sky and not to be underwater. I had listened to the inexorable advance of all of it through the hours I had lain awake in the lonely bed in the dim room that increasingly felt to me drenched with all the universe's hopelessness. When the lightning finally arrived, it seemed like happy company and I finally fell asleep.

In the morning it was still coming down. I set my saddlebags outside the door and stood surveying the scene from under the overhang. It was going to be a major drag loading the bike as it poured; I would have to put on my helmet just to keep my head reasonably dry. Suddenly I had an idea. I thought I could push the bike onto the walkway outside the door where it would be sheltered under the overhang. I went out into the wet and mounted the bike in order to rock it off the centerstand. I managed one or two heaves before I realized the opening in the low concrete wall before me was a few inches too narrow to permit the Lario through. I abandoned the attempt and got off to put the saddlebags on in the rain.

I had just come back through the door with the tankbag a second later when an instantaneous something's-wrong jolt hit me. The bike was on its side. I ran to it and hauled on its bars with all my strength. I even tried the method I had been taught in the Motorcycle Safety Foundation class, one they assured us could be applied by a petite old lady to pick up a Gold Wing. It didn't work for me. Whether or not it was actually happening, I imagined gas and oil and gear lube and battery acid flowing out of places it was never meant to flow from, and I was in a tizzy. My bike had never been down before. I looked wildly around, and that's when I saw that a van was parked next to the office; it was idling, for I could see exhaust pluming into the dampness. I ran over and knocked on the window. A startled man rolled it down. "My bike's fallen over!" I said breathlessly. "Please, could you help?" He sat there with exactly the same expression on his face. "It's just over there," I pleaded, and then he nodded slowly but still without moving. "Quickly!" I began to feel frantic. At last the door opened and he followed me. The two of us were able to raise the bike, and I thanked the speechless man several times, although I did not look at him: I was looking for damage to the Lario.

There was a slight scratch on the left valve cover, and another on the end of the clutch lever, which had not broken off as it easily might have. The handlebars seemed a bit lopsided, but everything turned and went in and out as it should. I switched on the ignition and hit the starter button with my gut clenched. The bike fired up as quickly as it ever had and held its idle perfectly.

Once on the road, I realized what had happened. I had rocked the bike around on the layer of gravel covering the soaked earth on which it was parked just enough to destabilize it thoroughly, and in the one second I was in the room several hundred pounds of assorted material fell over soundlessly. Something else took nearly to Wolfe Island to figure out. Why had that man been so slow to respond?

It turned out to be my fault in two senses. One, I had used the word *bike*. Two, I had been a woman. Ergo, he thought I had dropped my bicycle. He thought I was nuts.

The Jolly Roger Motel in Parry Sound, Ontario, was the other kind of motel, and the Chateau Marmont compared to the Bartlett Pair. Besides, the parking lot was a sumptuous array of colorful sportbikes and café racers, here for the ninth annual Sportbike Rally, a rally whose governing principle is an ironic sense of humor lightly dosed with Canadian politeness. Instead of giving long-distance and people's choice awards, it calls a spade a spade with the Cheap Awards, which bestow the Moto Whiner upon a world-class complainer, the Smoking Toe on a foolhardy fast freak, the Turf Luck on someone who goes down with style, and the Freshly Tuned Laurels on a bike that never seems to do the simplest things a bike was meant to do, such as start. The crowd is well scrubbed and could be easily mistaken for the audience at a college graduation. People are neatly attired in full leathers or cordura Aerostich suits, and they walk around admiring the often exceptional European and Japanese sportbikes that have come from both the United States and eastern Canada, including BMWs, Ducatis, Moto Guzzis, and a Bimota or two along with the buzzingly quick little two-stroke rice burners (not a term of derision) that aren't allowed in the United States because of emissions rules. In the evening folks retire to the so-called Yamahall to continue their bench-racing exploits and watch bike-related videos. The weekend's crown event is a dinner cruise around the Thirty Thousand Islands, before which the event's MC and guiding light, Mike Moloney, will thoughtfully provide small squares of wood to riders as they enter the parking lot. These they will place under kickstands so they won't return from the cruise to a sight like the one that greeted me outside the Bartlett Pair.

The morning after I arrived, I got up early, put on my riding gear, and went into the Jolly Roger's dining room. It was filled with motorcyclists, all of them ready to ride over to the rally site as soon as the breakfast eggs were dispatched. I felt a lump of self-pity in my throat when I saw that I was the only person who was alone. The other tables were filled with parties of two or three or four, all talking animatedly. And I knew that the cure was as simple as going up to any table with an empty chair and asking if I could sit down—motorcyclists are uniformly gregarious and welcoming. But that was to me also as simple as jumping out of a plane into the vertiginous sky: something I lacked the basic instinct to make myself do.

I sat down at the smallest table, put my helmet on the chair opposite, and consulted the menu for a moment. The beleaguered waitress came over, pad poised. "I'll have two scrambled eggs with rye toast," I said, "and a large cranberry juice." I handed back the menu and hoped the food would come quickly, for I always felt awkward eating alone in public.

As it happened, the food took a while, and the room had nearly emptied out when it arrived. But it was not an it, it was a them. The waitress carefully set down a plate of scrambled eggs and a glass of juice at the place across the table, and an identical order in front of me. "Actually, I only have room for one," I said and smiled. She looked perplexed. "I'm sorry, you're alone?" My nod confirmed the inconceivable to her: there was not a man for whom I was waiting, a man with a motorcycle. And she was not the only one who was sorry about that.

If ever I wish to test the elasticity of my consciousness by posing fundamentally unsolvable conundrums along the lines of "Try to conceive of infinity," I have only to recall the night I stopped at a highway tollbooth and held out my money. The toll taker, a guy in his twenties, fairly started blubbering. Finally he squeezed it out with incredulity in his voice: "Did you ride that motorcycle here all by yourself?"

Every woman who rides in this country has been asked that perspicacious question at least once, and some so often they now amuse themselves with thinking up commensurately smart rejoinders: "No, I carried it on my head." "You've heard of the Immaculate Conception? Well, it's sorta like that."

Two other first-person incidents, although I could certainly provide more:

I took my car in to the transmission specialists last week; naturally they recommended a complete replacement. Anyway, I whisper to the friend who's with me that the mechanic has an Italian accent. My friend says proudly, and loudly, to him, "She owns a Moto Guzzi!" The mechanic beams, starts talking about his Guzzi, now thirty years old, and about how he used to race a Gilera in Chile. I offer a few factoids in addition to nods and questions, and I tell him a bit about the Lario. He says parts for older Guzzis are not available here; I tell him I could get him a few names if he wanted. We proceed into the office, where I sign away my as-yet-unmade first fortune. I make one last comment about my 650, whereupon his eyebrows lower and he says, "*You* have a motorcycle?"

Every June, on Route 9 north of Keene, New Hampshire, the Christian Motorcyclists put up a wayside tent offering free coffee and sandwiches to riders bound for the races in Loudon who may be in need of stimulants, rest, or Jesus after a long trip. John and I pulled in from the road for a break, and I had just dismounted and was taking my helmet off when a couple of guys started heading toward me, as was John, after parking on the other side of the tent. They walked around the Lario a couple of times, looking it over, and waited for John to reach us before asking him, "How do you like this bike?" John merely smiled and said, "I don't know. You'll have to ask her, since she's the one who owns it." Whereupon the two asked John a few further questions; they never once addressed me.

Amusing as these episodes were, they and others like them have nonetheless prompted a more sober realization: Apparently the sight of a woman on a motorcycle so profoundly disturbs the way things are that even the eyes are not to be trusted. In turn, I have to shake myself and ask what year this is.

As it happens, it would not matter what year it is, since the proportion of female participants among motorcyclists in America has remained relatively constant since the beginning, ranging from about 7 to 12 percent. In other words, it would seem nothing much has changed in a hundred years. (The current figure I have heard for Germany is 20 percent, while for a country like Italy I suspect it may be lower even than ours.) In the same tradition as the news reports about motorcycling's "new," clean image that recur like clockwork every decade or two, word that women have finally breached the walls of "one of the last bastions of implied machismo," as a recent newspaper story put it, has been broadcast again and again over the years.

Little has changed. But why the persistence of this stasis? In any conversation about bikes and women, I encourage my interlocutor to float a theory for it. More than once I have heard: "Well, I guess it's because motorcycles have always been considered so *male*." That merely forms an elaboration of the original question. I want to know why motorcycles keep being considered so male.

In the late sixties, a Harvard Medical School psychiatrist named

Armand M. Nicholi II described a new mental malady: "motorcycle syndrome." The doctor's subjects were all obsessed with motorcycles, thought or dreamed about them constantly, and spoke forcefully of the incredible sense of power and strength riding conferred. It was, Nicholi felt, symptomatic of their "tenuous masculine identification." He had determined that many of them feared they might be homosexual and used a motorcycle to compensate for what they sensed as their effeminacy.

What would the doctor have done with Andrea, who averages twenty thousand miles a year on her BMW, would rather use it than a car to commute to work (against the wishes of her husband, also a rider), and tries to make at least one coast-to-coast round trip per year? Or with Erica, who discovered her affinity for bikes the minute she got on one, as well as her affinity for speed?—she picked up the bug so quickly after taking the beginning rider's course that she began to feel she was invincible and kept cornering quicker and quicker, until a week later when her Kawasaki KZ440 reached its maximum lean angle and spit her off in the middle of a turn. With a deepened respect for what bikes can and cannot do, she has moved up from a Guzzi V50 to a 750cc Ducati Supersport, which she rides like a demon. ("Look—it's a chick!" amazed onlookers have been heard to exclaim.) She has become addicted to racetrack riding classes, and is often one of the faster riders among the predominantly male enrollment. She cannot envision a life whose center is not firmly fixed on riding, and it seems inconceivable to her to date any man who is not equally enthusiastic, because she knows, if forced to choose between bike and man when riding season rolls around, which party will lose. What would the doctor do with these or any of the thousands of women—mothers, wives, grandmothers, lesbian and straight—who apparently do not need to reinforce their masculinity with it but still crave the undeniable rush of motorcycling?

What is it about women's partaking of this pleasure that seems so threatening? (Giving rise, no doubt, to the frequent backhanded compliment. This caption from a motorcycle book published in the sixties, accompanying an obvious example of the use of cheesecake to sell bikes, must stand in absolute mastery: "Many a male ego has been deflated by the skill of today's motorcycling miss. Attractive girls enjoy cycling, such as this young lady on a Jawa.")

And what is it about a woman riding a bike that is, at least in the abstract, always considered so sexy? Perhaps it is related to the same factor that causes men's obsessions with bikes to be considered evidence of suppressed homosexuality: their phallic nature. The hard, thrusting power delivered at groin level. For a female to usurp this kind of power must be seen as a transgressive act, one that toys with taboo. She's not *supposed* to have something like that between her legs.

At the same time, the persistent, leveling reduction of women on bikes to a single image of sexuality—oh boy, I bet she's ready to rock and roll underneath that leather—and especially the image of garage-calendar and advertising prop, draped over the chrome in her string bikini and trying to look as preorgasmic as it is possible to do in a drafty studio while fondling cold metal, castrates her of that daring appendage. She's not *really* doing anything with that machine, she's waiting for a guy; she's not using that power for her own pleasure, she's using it to give pleasure to someone else.

For every two people who express admiration for women who ride, and there are plenty, there is one who is disturbed by them. The perturbation can manifest itself in responses that range from a curious willed blindness all the way to edgy anger. An extreme example of the latter response was offered to a foreign woman who was at a small gathering of motorcyclists in Germany. She noticed that one strange man, his hair hanging in greasy strings, had fixed a glinty eye on her as she stood in the center of the group, sipping a mug of tea. Finally he teetered forward to put his face inches from hers, ignoring her stunned husband standing next to her. "You don't like motorcycles, do you?" he queried. "I ride one," she said. He leaned in closer and she stepped back. "Women can't ride. They're too weak." "Tell that to my bike." He pressed on: "It must be a small one." She was getting pissed now. "It's fast enough." He tried to laugh. "Fast enough for you to put it in a ditch." "Not once in the years I've been riding." She turned away, almost more disgusted with herself for getting that far into it with a lunatic. Her husband later opined that the guy was trying to pick her up. What a brilliant strategy, she thought.

Advertising, our preeminent disseminator of visual imagery, simultaneously reflects the way things are and promises a hopeful future that is yet to be. In the world portrayed in motorcycle advertising, the way things are is the way things are meant to remain. Only a couple of manufacturers routinely show women riding their machines. BMW is first among them, and when it presents the stock vision of two riders on a twisty two-lane through bucolic landscape, one of them is more often than not a woman. BMW has also run an unprecedented campaign in which only women appear, namely the three who in 1993 rode Bavarian iron twelve thousand miles to the Arctic to benefit a breast cancer foundation. It is no coincidence (though it is not clear whether the advertising preceded the reality or followed it) that BMWs have an especially large share of the female market here and are often enough the best-represented marque at gatherings of women riders. (Harley can make a similar claim, and its female constituency is of a size that can support the publication of a glossy magazine called *Harley Women*.)

It is thus a mystery why, for instance, when a few years ago Yamaha introduced the Seca II, an ideal mount for women—who sometimes must stage a desperate search for a lightweight, moderately powered bike that is not so tall they cannot reach the ground with their feet—its ads showed only men riding it, although sometimes with a woman as passenger. The question is begged on bended knee: Why do these manufacturers shoot themselves in the foot by refusing to market directly to an untapped 50 percent of potential buyers? The most common answer I have heard is one that betrays an unsavory truth: They fear any model that becomes popular with women would be shunned by men, the experience of Harley and BMW to the contrary notwithstanding. At any rate, with the status quo thus maintained, the motorcycle industry won't have to bother its pretty little head with worrying over the possibility that it is turning off female customers by, say, continuing to use half-naked women to sell its wares.

If you are looking for examples of women who possess large stores of mechanical ability, drive, and endurance when it comes to motorcycling, Theresa Wallach is a fine place to start. At seventeen, in 1935, she and a friend set off from London in a sidecar rig with the goal of reaching Cape Town. (Previously, she writes, she had found herself "staring wide-eyed at motorcycles instead of boys. My parents . . . told me that unless I settled down I would end up being nobody's bride.") They ended their journey after climbing the 3,550 feet of South Africa's Table Mountain, and by becoming the first women to cross the Sahara by bike.

In 1939 she rode a Brooklands lap of over 100 mph and was awarded the British Motorcycle Club's Gold Star, the only woman ever to win one. She also competed in trials and scrambles. When the war broke out, she joined a transport corps of the Women's Auxiliary Territorial Service, where she was issued a motorcycle as the first woman dispatch rider in the British army. Later in her service, now with the Royal Electrical and Mechanical Engineers, Wallach became the first woman to pass the mechanic fitter's test: " 'And who,' I remember saying, "could be more suited for the sensitive touch necessary for diesel nozzle hand-lapping?' "

After demobilization she and her motorbike took off for America, where in two and a half years she worked at eighteen jobs and rode 32,000 miles. Deciding to live in the States permanently, she did a stint as a bike mechanic, opened a motorcycle dealership, and started a rider instruction school. In 1970 she published *Easy Motorcycle Riding*, a concise and authoritative guide for the beginner. The cover of the paperback edition shows a man riding the bike with a woman as passenger.

The idea that women piloting their own motorcycles is perfectly natural, not to mention seemly, has proved difficult to impress in any lasting way on the popular consciousness. Indeed, the early decades of the sport seemed somewhat more sympathetic than the latter to the notion of women as riders of equal standing with men. As early as 1897, both the Coventry Motor and the Humber companies in England were making ladies' models; in the twenties, Harley-Davidson promoted some models as "The Woman's Out-Door Companion" ("the feature-refined, woman-kind Harley-Davidson.... If you are an out-door girl or woman you'll glory in the 'git' and the 'go' of motorcycling"). Also in the twenties, Pratts gasoline sought to be the fuel of choice for women riders. A British ad for it showed it knew whereof it spoke: "On the question of fuel the points which most appeal to the lady motor-cyclist are 'snappy acceleration,' 'pick-up,' 'mileage,' 'clean running' and 'easy starting.' That is why she always chooses Pratts Spirit." Those also happen to be, no more and no less, the points that appeal to men.

On the other hand there is the story of Della Crewe, a Waco, Texas, woman who in 1915 was touring the United States on her brand-new Harley; she was accompanied by her pooch, Trouble. Riding in northeastern Ohio in November, she met with seasonal bad weather. She sought shelter at a farmhouse, where she was at first refused by the angry farmer, who roundly—and, need I add, paternalistically—chastised her for being out on the snowy roads in the first place.

Sisters Betty and Nancy Debenham, the British authors of 1928's eminently sensible *Motor-Cycling for Women: A Book for the Lady Driver, Side-Car Passenger, and Pillion Rider,* show how a sense of humor is the most necessary auxiliary equipment (although they also recommend Burberry's motorcycle coats, Russian boots, and, in a pinch, a bit of whiskey poured into cold, wet footgear). On their maiden voyage with a sidecar rig through the countryside, they discovered the hard way that a combination uses more gas than a solo machine. Pushing it to the top of a hill, then coasting down into a small hamlet, they found a woman willing to sell them some spare petrol from a can, even though her husband was away. The tank filled, they kicked—and kicked and kicked and kicked. At last the lord of the manor came home and asked to hear the narrative of their misfortune. Not from the can behind the shed? he asked his wife. That was filled with leftover paraffin! The Debenhams upended the tank and at last filled it with real fuel. "This incident serves to show that it is a great mistake to buy petrol at wayside cottages and sheds," they noted in conclusion.

Women were equally drawn to the excitement of early automobiling, and more than a few proved adept drivers. In 1905, Mrs. Clarence Cecil Fitler won two races at Cape May, "loudly cheered by the thousands of spectators," said the *New York Times.* Joan Newton Cuneo, a well-known racer of the time, was the only woman driver competing in the first Glidden Cup, a thousand-mile event, also in 1905. Four years later she broke speed records in the Mardi Gras races in New Orleans and gave Ralph De Palma, the country's most famous male racer, quite a run. Later in that year—a coincidence?—the AAA banned women as drivers or even passengers in sanctioned events.

It is hard not to see such an organization as slumbering quietly until woken by the news that women are actually winning races from men; whereupon they hoist themselves to their feet and hurriedly declare women personae non gratae. Sometimes they would say it was for women's own protection, but since women had never asked to be protected but rather to be allowed to compete, the question arises as to who it was who required shielding.

Predictably, women who sought to enter motorcycling contests found the door-slamming disease rampant among these governing bodies as well. Although early on women were sometimes taking top honors—such as Muriel Hind, who in England in 1911 successfully raced a 6-hp Rex—the slightly delayed reaction to exclude them occurred with suspicious frequency hot on the heels of a win.

Clara Wagner, the fifteen-year-old daughter of the maker of Wagner motorcycles, was issued a membership card from the Federation of American Motorcyclists in 1907. Three years later she came in first on a 365-mile endurance run, earning a perfect score. Her win was quickly declared null; the trophy went elsewhere. The other participants in the race, fully aware of what she had accomplished, took up a collection to buy her a gold pendant instead.

Although she is now over eighty years old, Dot Robinson recently stole the show when she appeared in 1994's *She Lives to Ride*, a documentary film about women riders. She is shown mounting her pink Harley, with its lipstick case attached to the handlebars, to go to the golf course for a round with her lady friends. A charter member of the Motor Maids, who still ride in uniforms consisting of light blue shirts, white boots, and matching neckerchiefs, she is living proof that looks are deceiving, for she was the first woman to finish the Jack Pine Tour, a renowned and rugged five-hundred-mile endurance race that was held annually in northern Michigan. Together with her husband, Earl, she established a cross-country sidecar record (eighty-nine hours) in 1935, and she was forced to wage a war of wits with the AMA, which wished to deny official recognition of her achievements. Again, it was fellow competitors, those best situated to appreciate the true nature of a win, who assisted her cause, at her suggestion flooding the officials with so many letters decrying their stand they were soon led to rethink their position.

Lest their attitude appear a quaint memory of long-gone times, consider the case of Gina Bovaird, who in 1980 became the first woman to finish in the top ten at an AMA race. In 1971, officials had tried to throw her out of the pits when she was crewing for a friend, even though Kitty Budris had much earlier cracked the gender barrier for mechanics by receiving her AMA license in 1969 (and building a winning BSA racer). The following year, Bovaird tried to enter a race only to have her bike disqualified; *People* magazine reported that the same machine had placed second in that very race the year before. In 1979 she took the record for fastest novice—male or female—at Daytona: 141.66 mph.

The ability of women like Bovaird and Nancy Delgado, who currently campaigns a Honda 125 on the AMA pro circuit, to compete professionally despite the obstacles in this country is due to the battle fought by Kerry Kleid, a motocrosser. Although she had been given an AMA pro license in 1971, it was later confiscated—on the field—on the grounds that AMA rules did not permit women to race professionally. Kleid had to go to court to keep what was already hers, a testimony to the vehemence with which the status quo can be guarded. Now, Delgado said recently in an interview, "I am really excited about the fact that there are more and more women racing. . . . I think a lot of them needed to see someone else go out there and do it first, and now they are saying, 'I can do it too.' . . . We are entering an era when [women] aren't being held back by anything; the only ones stopping them [are] themselves."

I have almost lost count of the times I have been to the races in New Hampshire in June. Ever since we discovered the cabins by the lake, the visit has offered a good dose of quiet against the sometimes frenzied pace of merrymaking in the area. And ever since my first and last visit to Animal Hill, the patch of campground beyond the track where they used to allow such expressions of the fun-loving spirit as bonfires of Japanese bikes and an inflatable love doll hung by the neck and violated in every orifice by a whiskey bottle, I have learned where I am likely to have a good time and where I am not. Weirs Beach on Saturday night is not one of the former.

But when Bob, Mike, John, and Erica decided they wished to go where the action was, who was I to say no? Still, I was almost gleeful when the ignition on John's Moto Guzzi 500cc Monza decided to play hide and seek, not for the first time, when we were halfway there. We pulled into a parking lot, and while John checked wires and unrolled electrical tape, we watched the parade pass us by. A thick river of bikes was moving so slowly you had to admire the sense of balance exhibited by those who were two-up on monstrously heavy cruisers. They went by in a hail of shouts, some directed at Erica and me ("Tits! Tits!") and some at the moon.

When John had finally patched the power lines, we rejoined the passing stream. After another mile, Erica's V50 overheated and we had to stop again. This time it was next to a crowd of people standing around a flatbed truck parked on the shoulder; on it was a bank of spotlights trained on a piece of otherwise ordinary roadway. But it stood as proof that in some places all you have to do is set up a stage for a drama to materialize. After a few minutes of rather humdrum performance—attempts at rear-tire burnouts and shows of naked breasts ("It's amazing what you can get just for asking," cracked Bob) and hoots and howls—here it came. With a precision pounding of accelerator and brake at once, the driver of a Camaro managed to spin the car around once, lose control, and hang it on top of the guardrail on the opposite side, where it stayed, teetering. The crowd went wild.

We made it to our dubious destination at last, and after parking streetside in the Weirs, we ordered lobster rolls at a window and went to sit at an outdoor picnic table. The sidewalks were filled with bikers, laughing and eating and talking. Then I started the whole thing. Spoilsport.

My question was not entirely rhetorical: "What about making great amounts of smoke and noise is so much hysterical fun?"

John suggests it is the result of too much ego combined with an exhibitionist streak; that sounds wrong to me, and I make a case for its being instead utterly undeveloped ego. Bob has been silently eating until he fixes an eye on me and spits out, "That's the stupidest shit I've ever heard." He tears a chunk out of his sandwich and suddenly sets the whole thing down. He tells me he knows I love the attention when men howl at me, as do all the other women here, because look, they're having a good time, and this is all about fun, which if I can't appreciate I'm a loser. All I could think as he was speaking with such certainty was how all my life I have tried to avoid the feeling, when my body is commented on by strangers, of being scraped from inside, a painful sensation that I will do anything to avoid.

Much later, when we were out to dinner in New York one night, Bob said something—I forget what, but it was designed to provoke— that raised my temperature as surely as if he had turned a propane torch on me. I gritted my teeth and said to myself, Yes, he's wrong. Flamingly wrong. But you are not going to convince him of it, and you'll only have an idiotic fight and go home angry. "Gee, Bob, you may be right," I said out loud, and I was surprised to not suddenly find myself struck dead by agreeing to something I did not agree with. For good measure, anyway, I added to myself, In a pig's eye you are.

But that night in Weirs Beach, I began to cry.

I went to a gallery in SoHo to see an exhibition of works by Richard Prince. They were his usual thing of rephotographing photos from mass media, this time from a biker magazine, probably something like *Iron Horse*. They were based on those ineluctably sad photos guys send in of their girlfriends posing, draped over Harleys, in some grotesque, distant approximation of professional porn. Photographed again and blown up to many feet in size, the grain and bad color wash over you.

These are normal women in one way—they don't have perfectly rounded silicone-balloon breasts or model-fine faces; they mostly wear brittle dyed-blond hair in bad cuts and lurid makeup. But they are not normal in some other ways. They are colluding in their own debasement, and this is seen somewhere deep in their eyes, though their lips smile and their backs arch in feigned ecstasy.

Mainly they look uncomfortable (some of the poses are acrobatically painful) and tentative, as if they wished they could do something, *anything*, else to please the men behind the Instamatics—who themselves are caught in their grossness in some small photos, the kind designed to show everyone how wild-'n'-get-down the weekend party was. In fact, the parties look like desperate last stands, where only pots and rivers of beer could wash away some terrible discomfort. Might it be the ultimate discomfort, that of being conscious? It's clearly a habit, too, on grandly longstanding scale, given the enormous evidence of the male bellies. These American-iron diehards say, "We just like to kick back, just like to have our freedom," but it would be hard to picture a more manacled, helpless, compulsive segment of society. They are running, all right, but it is at a suspiciously frantic pace. It seems likely it is not to their freedom but away from themselves. If so, the price of the unconsciousness at which they end is the abdication of any remaining sense of responsibility. They become perennial children, subset class bully; their vigorously upheld motto is "Shit Happens." The ones who frequently get more than their share of the shit are their women, who must take off their clothes in public and pretend to like it in order to receive the brutish attention that is made to stand in for affection, respect, and regard in their world.

It had been years since I had first started experiencing the waves of panic that would inexplicably wash over me at the strangest times— as I was watering the plants, as I sat down to dinner. A dense whiteness would appear in front of my eyes, my heart would pound, nausea would knead my gut, and a sensation like being on an elevator plunging dozens of stories would sometimes bring me to my knees. I would go stand in a hot shower, for some reason the only place that could talk me down from the cliff a bit and dampen the weird buzzing I heard in my ears, and I would put my cheek against the wall and sob. Years later, I can still call up every detail of the small white-flecked blue tiles with their somewhat odorous old grout. I did not understand what was happening to me or why, only that it was terribly odd to simultaneously fear death with such ferocity and beg for it to arrive quickly. I had to force myself to go out and ride, just as sometimes I had to force myself to go the three blocks to the grocery store. As often as not, the fear (or the Fear, as I called it, since it exhibited all the signs of a malicious independent being) would glide effortlessly from my body to that of my motorcycle. Then it was not I who had a terminal condition, but the Lario. It would be breaking down any minute; it would be no simple matter, either, but burned valves, thrown rods, expectorated spark plugs, or just an inexplicable cessation of all power. On some especially grand occasions, I would be riding along through the beauteous world pressed by the heavy certainty that both of us were dying at once.

Naturally, something as insistent as the Fear had dibs on my heart. After years of semidisastrous dating, including two truly awful years during which I tormented myself by longing for the love of a man who was brilliant at stringing one along but never quite coming through, I decided the romance racket was not for me. It was quite a relief. No more would I have to hope, wonder, fret. No more would I keep half an eye out at all times for a likely candidate. It was not going to happen, and that was that. I could at last devote all my energies to work, one area at least in which I could determine my fate.

That very week, I decided to move forward on every possibility for advancing my career that I could think of. There was freedom in industriousness. I made phone calls, submitted manuscripts, wrote letters. One was to a writer, already successful in the way I wished to be, with whom I had a vague connection. Perhaps he could give me some advice. When I called to follow up, he graciously agreed to meet me one afternoon in a coffeehouse in the East Village.

How simple the gesture.

Luc and I got married in southwestern Massachusetts, because we wanted the expansiveness of the countryside to witness the event, and because we had found a beautiful old inn with a Normandy-style barn in which to have the reception. I had landed what I could only consider the perfect man. But like Persian rugs which intentionally bear some small imperfection so as not to presume to godlike faultlessness, he had one offending thread: he did not ride. During the year of our courtship, I rode far less than in any year since I first bought a motorcycle, succumbing most weekend mornings to the Velcro effect of a bed that contains a compelling reason to stay there.

When I did manage to tear myself away, I still relished the sights I came across on my rides, but I was always nagged by the feeling that I had left something behind. I found myself aching to have him there just so I could say, "Over there—look!" Then there were other matters: my riding companions were almost always men, and it now felt strange to share a motel room with another man, no matter how innocently. Money was now our money, and I suffered guilt in taking it for my solitary vacations, when he refused to do the same for himself. I grew to long to encounter just one other woman in the same situation, but instead I found women who would exclaim, "How could you possibly be with a man who doesn't ride? I couldn't imagine it." (I have never heard a man utter a similar sentiment, perhaps since many men seem either to accept or rather like the fact that their spouses don't come along for the ride.)

But time works with solid predictability. A few years into married life, it didn't seem like such a bad idea to get away alone every now and again, although I know I still would like to unweave this particular minor asymmetry in my mate and substitute another.

Last summer we realized my second-fondest dream by renting a house in the country, in a rolling landscape of cow pastures and forests assiduously reclaiming stony farms from previous centuries. A significant component of this dream, along with the desire to garden and to substitute a world of sounds richer to me than the urban ecosystem's radios and shouting into the night, had been the wish to dispense with the tortuous rigmarole that accompanies attempts to get out of New York City for a summer ride. After an hour of tongue-biting traffic, you'd still only be at Bear Mountain, and for the hundredth time would zing around the same few miles of curves with a horde of other bikes. Then you'd have to turn around and fight your way back to town. In place of that, I had delirious visions of clear roads that began where my driveway ended; perhaps it was a sign that I had truly begun aging, that inability to suffer petty inconveniences and not care.

Once I discovered, through nervous trial and error as well as welcome advice, how to get up and, worse, down the long, steep, and very rocky dirt driveway (keep it moving on the way up, but smoothly; not too slowly and relying on the BACK BRAKE ONLY, FOR CRISSAKES! on the way down), there I was. Road heaven.

Up in Delaware County I dusted off the reason I loved bikes. Giving shape to the air you then cut, happening onto the wellspring of primal rhythm. At around six the light would be perfect, and I'd say, Bye, back in an hour, and I'd fly down the hills and give myself pop quizzes on corners, trying to keep everything smooth and accelerating out of the turn, and go "Mooooo" whenever I passed some cows, as has been my ritual since I first started riding. I also worked on trying to make peace with a secret, not too conscious wish to find someone who would take care of my-bike-and-by-extension-me, because I discovered in this a dangerous futility that only served to keep alive in me a pervasive sense of incompetence. I was to do this by at last considering some of the incontrovertible evidence I had accumulated over the years that no one was as omnipotent as I kept hoping, or at the least that others' competence was usually lower than I expected while mine was somewhat higher. It had become a bad habit with me, manifested in a repeated cycle of entrusting my bike to a series of new mechanics—whom I had all invested, daddylike, with supreme knowledge—then standing by while they screwed things up and charged me for it. I'd have to put things right when I got home. I was also trying to get a seriously wedged but now all too glossy memory of Franz from my mind, who had no business being there. I began to sense that my motorcycle was again trying to tell me something, this time something ancient and wise. What was that I heard? *Oh, shit.* Yes, I thought so. What's that now? *Own ship.* I don't understand. *Captain.* Captain who? *Captain your own ship.* Ah, thanks.

Erica's fervent proselytizing on behalf of the racetrack class she had taken could not at this time have found a more willing convert. She had also passed along the information that Reg and Jason Pridmore, the father-and-son racers who created and run the CLASS Motorcycle Schools at racetracks around the country, would be offering the first all-female edition in July, under the auspices of the Women's Motorcyclist Foundation. Since almost every motorcycle event is pretty much an all-male event by default, I was intrigued by the possibility of not feeling so minority-member at one. And I wanted to see what made Erica, and John in his more subdued manner, unable to convey much more than a dazed happiness in trying to describe CLASS.

The slogan of the Motorcycle Safety Foundation is "The More You Know, the Better It Gets," and CLASS turned it into a truism. The feeling of confidence derived from knowing exactly what to expect of your machine and your combined capacities and limitations effectively deletes the element of abject fear that accompanies the desirable activity of throwing yourself into a curve, leaving only the "ah"-provoking rush. The three of us had taken the MSF's Experienced Rider course in upstate New York two summers before, and getting good instruction and practice on panic braking and controlled skids can make for a very sweet sleep. That and having had a stupid bias (to indulge a redundancy) exposed and crushed, as our instructors were bearded, leather-vested Harley riders, and one of their bikes even sported ape-hanger handlebars and the sort of accouterments I associated with dangerous behavior. I will never again think such thoughts after having watched Bill McGuire on his extravagant chopper, arms above his head and feet stuck out in front, slice a line through the cones so precise you could draw it with a compass.

In July I paid my two hundred dollars, outfitted the Lario with new tires as instructed by the CLASS registration materials, and lit off once more for Loudon, New Hampshire. In contrast to every other trip I had made there, this one was a pleasure from the very second I departed, since I did so from the country. About ten miles from the house, I would make a right turn onto lovely Route 23 and stay with it for a hundred miles, until the Mass Pike and the mindless rush. Just before the Massachusetts state line I would be treated to a real "Top o' the world, Ma" sight, as the road climbs and turns, climbs and turns, suddenly to pull the curtain away and say, There. There spread below you is a distance-slewing panorama of vast plain that sifts off into vapor at the remote horizon. A bit farther on I would ride through Great Barrington, where I would wave at the restaurant in which three years earlier I had had my wedding rehearsal dinner, although there had been no actual rehearsal. As I flashed by on the bike, I had the feeling that I was passing by myself, forever leaning over my mother to give her a teary kiss, forever caught at the moment of being photographed wearing a sleeveless black top and diaphanous olive skirt.

The Bricktower Motel in Concord, hard by the highway, had been recommended by the Pridmores. It also offered a discount to participants in the class, which was really all the recommendation I needed. As I pulled up in front of the office, another woman was just coming out. Before she got back on her late-model BMW bearing a Michigan plate, she introduced herself; it was pretty obvious we were here for the same reason. I could have kissed Phyllis, for that was her name, because if she hadn't said anything to me, I might not have said anything to anyone for the duration of my stay. My gratefulness is puerile, I know, but there you are.

The desk gave me the key to the room next to Phyllis's, and after we took our bags into the rooms we sat down on the curb next to our bikes (ah, bliss) and watched the further arrivals. They came on a variety of machines, though more on high-mileage BMWs than any other kind, and in pickups hauling trailers. There were cruisers and there were sportbikes, and much that was in between. It was, to me, a sight to behold: for once I was not swooning over mechanical marvels, but over the people who rode them. I had no idea I had missed the mythic sisterly bonding experience as much as I apparently did.

When men get together at a motorcycle event, they talk fairly ceaselessly about minutiae—tires, performance, mechanical secrets, endless variations on the "one time when I was . . ." theme. When women get together at a motorcycle event, I discovered in New Hampshire, they talk about tires, performance, mechanical secrets, and endless variations on their pleasures as delivered by bikes.

After the class the next day, as we were relaxing around the Bricktower's small pool, feeding mosquitoes and waiting for the delivery of pizza and Chinese food, I counted perhaps a few more tattoos than would occur in your basic sampling of American women. As I had sussed out during a noisy Mexican dinner at a restaurant in Concord the night before, many of the women were lesbians, though I made more than a few erroneous identifications (no doubt because of my lack of what a friend calls gaynar, which is sort of like sonar only different). The disproportionate showing was due to the participation of two gay clubs, the Sirens of New York and Boston's Moving Violations. The rest of us were a motley collection with vaguer affiliations, like me and like Phyllis, a school social worker who with her husband also taught Motorcycle Safety Foundation classes, and who was here on her first extended bike trip alone. One woman, on a shiny new Harley, had obviously been encouraged to attend by her boyfriend, since he seemed bent on a vicarious experience. He stood just off in the wings during the entire day, occasionally running over to adjust something on her bike or give some sort of pep talk as if she were making her stage debut. She looked as chastened as a kid whose parent insists on coming on the daytrip to the carnival even though all the other kids get to go alone. Her growing embarrassment made the air surrounding her visibly heavier.

I learned at dinner that one woman was a truck driver; another taught engineering; one had just started racing—and winning— enduros, long-distance off-road races; another was sixty if she was a day and had butched hair that was dyed orange, green, blue, yellow, purple, and red—the rainbow that is the symbolic plea for sexual tolerance and that appeared in decal form on many windscreens and helmets. There were several couples, who between them had many, many bikes. As I sat back and watched some of these women, I wondered about the act of bravery that simply traveling with their partners was forced to become, and about the verbal and sometimes physical attacks nearly all of them had experienced. I imagined these utterly normal happy faces, now engaged in eating enchiladas and telling stories and asking questions, suddenly screwed up in the kind of anger and pain that comes from deep in the gut.

As it was to prove in New Hampshire that weekend, my penchant for sitting on a curb and absentmindedly glancing over the Lario sometimes had its additional benefits. There was the day I had ridden away from Franz's shop on an errand. I was cruising onto the highway when I felt this dropping-off of power. The tank was full of gas, and the petcocks were on; what was the problem? Just by luck, there was an exit coming up, and I managed to get halfway down the ramp before the engine died. I coasted to the bottom, where I wheeled the bike into a Pep Boys parking lot. I called Franz from the pay phone, and when he could offer no probable diagnosis from a distance, he told me to sit tight.

I did so on the curb outside the store, while people coming and going cast three-second glances of bemusement my way. Waiting with my chin in my hands to hear the sound of the rescuing 850 drawing near, I stared at the center of the bike as if it ought to reveal at least one small mystery of the universe. And so it did. Earlier in the day Franz had replaced the fuel line. This tubing is made of the kind of rubber whose disintegration acts as an accurate gauge of the level of atmospheric ozone, which—take it from me and the rubber items in my life—is growing dramatically worse. I suddenly saw how the length of the new lines was too great for the rather compressed space between tank and carb; they had folded, cutting off the flow of gas. I got out my Swiss army knife, trimmed a few inches from the petcock ends of the line, and all was right with the world once more. Too bad Franz was already on his way.

Now, on Friday night, as Phyllis and I sat chatting, my eye stopped on a dime-size spot of fresh liquid under the bike. I didn't have to dip my finger in it to know it was gear lube, a 90-weight oil finished with enough molybdenum to make it steel-gray and slippery as hell. When I lay down with my head just forward of the rear wheel, I saw it was emerging, slowly, from where the gearshift mechanism disappeared into the case. Shit. I had no idea what it meant. But I did not like leaks of any sort, especially since the previous one—in the final drive box, which had started on that last happy tour of the Blue Ridge—had gone misdiagnosed as overfilling until one day two months later, on a ride with Armen, when after I had stopped at a light the bike refused to go forward at the right time. As Armen found when he took it apart, water had gotten in from somewhere to displace the lubricating fluid until at last the pinion bearing cried uncle. And leaks, besides betraying a sloppy attitude toward machinery, also pushed my badly bruised panic button.

In New Hampshire, though, there was realistic cause for worry, since in the morning our bikes would go through a tech inspection before class to determine whether they were track-worthy. The instructors would be looking at tire treads to make sure at least 90 percent remained; at brake pads for wear; and for the absence of leaks, because that slippery stuff could give someone a nasty fall.

As soon as they saw me on my back under a bike, sympathetic female bystanders were asking if they could help. A few names were mentioned as belonging to particularly able mechanics. One of them, Barbara Ann Mahoney of the Sirens, was called over to take a look. I explained that I had changed the gear lube the day before leaving; it had been due for its five-thousand-mile replacement. Well, if it's like the BMW, she said, the problem is probably a seventy-five-cent gasket that's a snap to replace. She pointed out the shift linkage on her bike, which went squarely into the side of the gearbox. Looked easy enough to me.

That made it a natural, therefore, for the later discovery that its situation on the Guzzi at the rear underside of the case, close in front of the swingarm, necessitated a good twelve hours of rather complicated disassembly to get at. Leak it would. Meanwhile I would hold my breath during the inspection.

The next morning Phyllis and I stumbled out from our respective rooms shortly after the sun rose. We crossed the street in a sleepy haze for Dunkin' Donuts' quart-size cup of coffee, then we suited up and rode onto the highway in a dense fog. She was following me, because I purported to know my way to the raceway, but radar tracking would have stood her in better stead in the billowing whiteness, the thickest I'd ever ridden through. Still, it would be hard to miss the two-story-tall signboard above the entrance to the New Hampshire International Speedway. It was odd to be here in this silence.

We rode past the gate and down through the tunnels under the track, emerging up the hill and through the gate in the storm fence surrounding the pit area. The rows of large sheds that on race days comprised a hundred different intent pods of team activity were all empty except for one, and it was filling up with women. Soon each was bent over her motorcycle, removing rearview mirrors, disabling brake lights.

When at last we were all seated in an array of folding chairs, Reg Pridmore stood up before us. As a London transplant who had won three AMA Superbike championships in the seventies, he knew, it could be presumed, plenty about riding. But what had made CLASS such a success, with some participants returning for twenty or thirty sessions (at a few hundred bucks a pop, including the cost of greatly increased consumption of sneakers, as Armen terms the often expensive tires), was a rather amazing gift for communicating that knowledge. His lessons rationed humor, succinctness, authority, and clear-eyed logic in the right measure, and watching him work was somewhat like watching a TV chef. As he enumerated the several rules that were intended to keep us from doing each other in on the track, he made you understand their grave necessity without further ado. He specified the first principles of good riding technique, said he would always emphasize smoothness over everything, for smooth riding defines good riding, and then turned the proceedings over to his son.

It was not really ironic that twentysomething Jason Pridmore was teaching us about good riding, which is equivalent to safe riding, while his lower leg was encased in one of those science fiction scaffoldings that you don't want to stare at very long, because it causes you to think overly much about whether those rods are actually disappearing into the skin. After all, it is not possible to race successfully without getting hurt; another way to look at it was to suppose that he would have been in a full body cast instead had he not been tutored by his father.

Since our group, numbering about forty, was smaller than usual, the instructors proposed running us in a single group rather than two self-graded slow and fast sections that would alternate. They explained we would all get more track time that way. A loud moan went up from one side of the audience, and a few women raised their hands in protest. No, separate us! they called. These were people who didn't want anyone in their way.

They got their wish, but that meant the slower of us would go first. We paraded out past the pit wall, and there I was, on the ribbon of pavement where I had first seen what had appeared to me as miracles.

At first, turn one seemed so much farther away than you would think, the homestretch in front of the grandstands nearly endless, but lap after lap it crept steadily up and up. The first lap was the easiest, and it was never the same after that. Every trouble with my riding technique that I had managed to hide under the rug for ten years came out to trip me. Downshifting proved my Waterloo. I had been doing it wrong, dreadfully wrong, all these years—trying to slow down to match engine speed to that of gear before gearing down, throttling off as I clutched and shifted, then bracing myself for the inevitable lurch as the new gear engaged at a different speed from the engine's. It had caused my body to assume an unconscious state of anticipatory clenching all the while; I had thought it would be unduly hard on the engine to make it suddenly rev up so hard at every downward shift. The good instructor-cops were on me in a second, and I heard the screaming whoosh of a Honda VFR 750 come up beside me; the instructor raised his left hand as he did so, and I followed suit, indicating to anyone behind me that I would pull off into the pit lane after the final turn.

"Are you fairly nervous out there?" he asked when we stopped. No, not especially, I wanted to say; you should see me when I really get upset! "I can read it in your back," he went on. "Why don't you concentrate on relaxing your upper body and using your lower body to guide the bike, like Jason said?"

After a few more laps we were called in, and the squid kids—racer wannabes—were let out of the pen. To their bikes' distant reverberate tune, we took in the first lesson: keeping revs up and speed on a smooth arc through downshifting. We were also told, the next time we went out, to think about the fact that the friction point on the clutch was much farther out than we thought—requiring only a fraction of the time and effort we had been expending on hauling the lever all the way in to the bar. Sure enough, I had long ago forgotten something I once knew. Without thinking too much about it, I now shaved a few minutes off every subsequent lap, shifting that much quicker.

And so it went through the day. Every lesson seemed designed to address my particular deficiencies, and every new track session simultaneously presented a further problem that required work and offered the sweet feel of slightly deeper, faster cornering. The chicane before the straightaway became my favorite, the bike doing a swift left-side, right-side curtsy through the tight S. It really worked, as Reg said, to listen to the machine: it would not steer you wrong. When it started to complain, though, and caused you to apply muscle, something was going amiss. And the lesson could go hard.

It was exhausting. But by the afternoon I had climbed over my own personal obstacle course to get to what was pretty much the middle of the group: I was not passed too often, and I passed a few others myself. I glanced at my tires after one of the last sessions to note with incredulity the wear mark all the way to the edge of the tread. It seemed the bike was leaning about as far over as possible before the pegs scraped the ground, although a fraction less to the right; nearly everyone has one side on which cornering goes a little tougher than the other.

After taking twenty or thirty of these classes, I figured, I might be a pretty fair rider. As it was now, I had an unbelievably powerful headache doing bench presses in my skull. All we had left was the "graduation ceremony," at which we would receive certificates of completion. In turn, the Women's Motorcyclist Foundation would present Reg Pridmore with a plaque to honor the risk he took in committing to try an all-woman group, one that could have cost him a lot of money, as the track fee remained the same regardless of the number of registrants he had. They also gave him a chocolate cake and a fairly in-tune rendition of "Happy Birthday," followed by an emotional commendation of one of the participants, who had fought the breast cancer that was one of the foundation's prime targets. We were all feeling like the kind of big, happy family whose members could only be unrelated, and we positively busted with pride when the instructors told us—no fooling—that we were the best class they had ever taught. And certainly, there had been no mishaps that day, as happened often enough in other classes. The instructors told us that there were always some guys among the students who sit through the same list of proscriptions we had heard, then go out on the track and proceed to pass someone on the inside in a corner, just like a real racer, and bring him down, not like a real racer. They also informed us that collectively we had improved more than any other batch, largely because we actually listened to what we were told to do and then went out and did it.

All the way home the Pridmores' words played on a tape loop in my mind, and I attempted to steer the bike using no pressure from my upper body, to relax the aforesaid, and to keep the revs up. I was patting myself on the back until I narrowly missed becoming car wax while making a left turn in which I neglected to remember that my general impatience did not equip me to see through delivery trucks.

I also spent time thinking about how wonderful it would be to take a trip with some other women. No more requiring my husband to suffer so much (I had only to imagine what I would be feeling as he waved goodbye on his way to spend a weekend with ten thousand women). On the other hand, I had to wonder what assumptions and bad manners two women arriving at a motel on motorcycles might provoke. Of course, I could be wrong. And this could be the best of all possible worlds after all.

Although you would not know it from attending some of the largest gatherings of motorcycles in the country, black people ride bikes, too. And they have for a long time. The late Bessie Stringfield, known as the Motorcycle Queen of Miami and who still rode at over seventy years of age, is the first black woman to have toured the lower forty-eight, which she did, incredibly enough, in the thirties. And look at the antepenultimate photograph in the American edition of Robert Frank's great work *The Americans*: well, it does no good to describe it. Just look.

As it is for blacks and whites in most aspects of American life, black and white motorcyclists live in essentially separate worlds that only seem to be one. I have lately been corresponding with a man named Hilton Webb, Jr., who currently resides in Attica Correctional Facility. I do not know what he's in for, and I don't want to, although as time goes on I suspect I will. What I do know is that he's articulate, thoughtful, black, and a biker. Here is part of his take on the subject:

> Most of my experience on the road has been as a GDI (goddamned independent) with but a few forays into group riding. Although I've done Sturgis and the cross-country thing it was solo. The times when I rode with large groups, most were all white with me as the "token" black. I can remember riding on only two occasions with black bikers. Both times were in the middle seventies and with the same club, namely the South-Side Shifters (so named because of the jockey shift low on the left side of their chopped hogs) out of East New York. [One time we joined] a much larger group out of South Philadelphia called appropriately the Wheels of Soul. It was the only time in my life . . . when my color on the back of a Harley-Davidson wasn't unique. There were about ninety of us and we rode to Big Daddy's on Long Island and partied a Labor Day weekend away. . . . It seems that being a black biker in America isn't far from being a black man in America.
>
> I've been all over this country and find that the black rider is subjected to racism from a large part of the one-percent crowd as well as the people who ride in tons of steel.
>
> I guess blackness is something that you have to be born into and live. The reactions are subtle; the tightened grasp on a pocketbook, the sideward glance, the helpful store attendant. As a biker, Denny's wasn't happy with my appearances, but when you're 6' 1" and 250-plus people have a tendency to keep their racist attitudes undercover unless they're drunk and in a crowd from which they can draw a spine.

If I could give a present to every woman rider in the world, it would be a videocassette of a 1988 Australian movie, *Shame*. Not that it's a cinematic work of art; it's a moral message movie, no matter how adroit a one, in the same mold as the western from which it derives its plot, *Shane*. It's just that the message and its mode of delivery have special resonance for female bikers.

Asta Caddell is a barrister on holiday, via a 750cc Suzuki Katana. After a late-night run-in with a ditch (better, she decides quickly, than with the large critter in the road), she repairs to the nearest small town. Over the days she pieces her motorcycle together again—declaring the rationality of engines a relief in contrast to people—she discovers the disturbing reason behind the queer silence of the town's womenfolk and the boorish insolence of the men. And you know the rest.

While the tale has an admirably feminist slant, the real gift to women is its suggestion of what to do when smirking men ask for a ride. Asta Caddell shows how to give them one.

# EIGHT

*"Now come on. Tell me, did you or didn't you ride my motorcycle off the
bedside table?"*
*This took Ralph by surprise. He had not expected the boy to guess
what happened. "Well, yes. I guess you might say I did," confessed Ralph,
rubbing his aching muscles.*
*"I thought so." Neither the mouse nor the boy was the least bit surprised
that each could understand the other. Two creatures who shared a love for
motorcycles naturally spoke the same language.*
—*Beverly Cleary,* The Mouse and the Motorcycle

Here is the single most upsetting thing that has happened to
me in ten years and tens of thousands of miles of riding
motorcycles.

Like any often-repeated thing, the annual trip to New Hampshire
in June has become laced with ritual. Since discovering it on that first
trip with Bob, I would make sure, either on the way up or the way
back, to take the scenic route that cuts east–west across southern
Vermont and New Hampshire. By the time it is about twenty miles
west of Brattleboro and the Connecticut River, Route 9 has climbed
two thousand feet farther up into the piney mountains. A few miles
before the Green Mountain National Forest begins, at the top of
Hogback Mountain, there is an old-fashioned tourist turnout featur-
ing a shedlike store selling every form of maple sugar product conceived by man, along with the type of cheap "gift" (rubber tomahawk,
highway bingo) that is my favorite, since they are among the handful
of things in the world that have remained unchanged since my child-

hood. It also houses, in the back, a display of stuffed wildlife so wrenchingly sad I could only look once.

There is a wooden-railed overlook from which you can view the trees of three states through the old magnifying viewer for the price of a quarter, or you can put a camera with a timer on the railing and then run and stand at the end with your traveling companion's arm around you to get a portrait of the two of you with the space dropping off magnificently behind. Up the hill across the street is a restaurant in a stone house with large picture windows; it serves marvelous pancakes and is not owned by a chain conglomerate—yet.

This must-stop is situated right at the apex of a blind curve in the road, a perfect half circle whose ends are prematurely obscured by forest. There are parking areas just off both sides of the road, meaning that cars are backing into and pulling off from the middle of this arc and pretty much leaving it up to God that nothing will be barreling around the corner.

One day I had finished my obligatory trinket shopping, including some maple sugar boy-and-girl figures for the friend who was taking care of my now-beloved cat, Bill, and I was sitting on the Lario with its front tire on the line separating parking lot from road. I looked to the end of the curve on the right, waited for a slow-moving station wagon to pass from the left, looked right again, and, seeing both sides clear, started left. My front tire had now just reached the double yellow line and I was about to cross over it into the right lane when, in a roar and a flash, four sportbikes appeared leaning all the way over from the right. They must have been going fifty or sixty around a corner that was good at prayerful best for thirty. My reflex was to increase my lean, too, so I would ride down the center stripe until they passed; they would still have the full lane to themselves. If I had been a passenger car, all of them would have gone splat.

My nerves were pudding for miles after that. But these fellows, who had thought nothing of blazing around a blind curve at supersonic speed, had now slowed down to forty. Even I went faster than that on a good straight bit. I was puzzled, but I figured maybe they were being friendly and were in the mood to meet another motorcyclist also enjoying this lovely day. I pulled ahead of one of them, and he yanked suddenly on the throttle to jump in front of me again. I got the message. They were pissed as hell and wanted to have a little talk.

I could imagine it well: You fucking goddam bitch, you almost killed us back there. What the hell were you doing pulling out in front of us?

I like confrontation about as much as stepping in discarded gum on a hot day in new shoes. But if I liked it better, I could have matched them ire for ire: What the fuck did you think you were doing going that fast on a road like that? I wish there *had* been a Volvo in my place, just to see how good you look hanging from the back bumper. There's not much more you can do before turning onto a road than wait until you can see no traffic coming from either direction, you jerks.

Instead I dropped my speed steadily. There were still forty miles of Vermont left in which I could frustrate their need for speed so badly they'd give up. The length of time to which they stuck at thirty on road they could have taken at eighty was testimony to their anger. But finally they peeled away, no doubt to tell the story to this day about the time a stupid girl almost took them down.


You were expecting perhaps a tale of depravity that would ice your soul? I often feel as though I disappoint those who like a bit of blood drama in their biking tales. Except for evidence of the grotesque, shriveled hate that resides in a certain portion of the American psyche and is sometimes on open display at rallies (T-shirts for sale read "AIDS Cures Fags,"

FAT CHICKS

"Speak English or Get the Fuck Out"), I can offer none. But I could tell you a little about the weird way small microcosms of near-perfect human society spontaneously arrange themselves around certain objects.

Not every biker is an angel, or a Hell's Angel. Yet in only two social groups of my acquaintance have I found an abundance of people who on the sole basis of a tenuous connection would, say, spend an entire day helping you out with some problem with no expectation of recompense. One is a small subset of the dog owners in my neighborhood, who will come pick up a fellow dog owner if she needs a ride, cancel their own plans in order to spend all morning helping search for a lost dog, or lend some cash to a near stranger, so long as he has a dog. The other is the worldwide brotherhood of Moto Guzzi riders. Both of these stand in for the small village of uniformly trustworthy good neighbors we seem to crave, the tribal life of all for one and one for all that is now simply apocryphal for most of us. As the French authors of *Toute La Moto* put it, "If all the guys in the world would pass each other the number 14 wrench . . . How often have we dreamed of this utopia? Well, it exists in the world of biking. Not always, not systematically, there's trash just as in every other milieu, but it exists nevertheless."

The *New York Times* reviewer of the documentary *She Lives to Ride* complained, "The film's composite image of these women is, in fact, so benign that cycling is painted almost as a kind of vigorous alternative to playing bridge or canasta." But that's really it! That's about as close to the truth of the experience as you can get for the great majority of motorcyclists, although Friday-night poker might be a better comparison—it more aptly recalls biking's inherently social, ritualistic aspects as well as its risk of valuable stakes, without which it might as well be Go Fish.

Loyalty, as we know, is earned, not free. You can't shout at schoolkids that they must love their country or their parents; you may get automatons frightened into mouthing the corresponding platitude, but you don't get the fealty-unto-death that can only be the result of a reciprocal experience of valuing and being valued.

The fact that among motorcyclists the loyalty can be fierce, sometimes more so than toward flag or blood, tells you something about what really goes on in motorcycling's sphere. There is brand loyalty, the kind that inspires bikers (and not just Harley fanatics, either) to have the logo of their favorite mount permanently inscribed on their flesh with ink. There is loyalty to the club, which can lead to deadly rumbles (of words or weapons) with outsiders as well as extraordinary acts of kindness to fellow members. There is loyalty to the object, which causes what is really just an assemblage of manmade parts to be given care that many living creatures do without, and even on occasion pride of place in the living room. There is loyalty to the abstraction, to "motorcycling," demanding a final expression such as that made in 1956 by the twenty-seven-year-old founder of Akron's Lots-A-Moshun biking club, who was buried with his riding jacket and license plate and escorted to the cemetery by a long cortege of cyclists; many a rider before and since has been laid to rest clutching the photograph of a beloved bike, even if it was the one that helped dig the grave. There is the loyalty that may well mask a fear, such as the common insistence that nothing depressing, upsetting, or unfavorable ever be uttered about the activity. (The alacrity with which motorcyclists close ranks on this issue is indeed suspicious. One might ask if cycling is so formidable, what does it matter if someone writes a word or two about its dark side? After all, as a human construct, it cannot help but have one.)

Then there is the finally inexplicable loyalty built of love.

Perhaps commerce has a heart after all. That would explain why the annual commercial motorcycle show, which travels the country and comes to New York City's Jacob K. Javits Convention Center, is timed so that it will illuminate the bleakest days of winter.

The convention hall hangs on the edge of the city, as on a rock cliff before the infinity of ocean. Something so huge, and so devoid of personality, could only be placed on a discarded nail clipping of Manhattan previously peopled solely by delivery trucks and the hidden business of railroads. Because this is the highlight, or only light at all, of the cold season for those who love bikes, you expect to come upon Eleventh Avenue as you would come upon Oz, beckoning green light irradiating the site. Yet the icy cubes of this glass mono-lith reflect only the sky above, and the place, blocks long and wide, seems abandoned on a Friday night in February.

But it is merely that the activity is concentrated, and you have to enter the proper door or else cross vast and lonely steppes of lobby before you can gaze down through plate glass onto the busy scene in one of the hundreds of convention halls within the convention cen-ter. One floor below, a room is alive with a million arrows of light shot from chrome. But this is not the true source of the frisson that runs through your body. Rather it is the giddy sight of so many motorcycles indoors, parked on carpet.

Thousands of people will turn out to see the latest models, which are usually very much like the previous year's models, but bowing to the fine tradition of marketing's manipulation of desire, the ever-new paint schemes and continual refinement of nonessential baubles (a new mirror design that amplifies the bike's mean-insect look, say, or the arbitrary replacement of last year's transparent smoked wind-screen with this year's opaque plastic) create instant lust for *this very one*. There are large displays of new wares from Honda, Yamaha, Kawasaki, Suzuki, Harley-Davidson (Hardly-Dangerous, says Armen); off-road, dual-purpose, sportbikes, cruisers, ATVs. The big tire manufacturers, like Metzeler and Avon and Dunlop, offer carousels of tires and glossy pamphlets, and the makers of lubricants like BelRay and Spectro are out in force. In the center of the hall, BMW commands attention with an eighteen-wheel semi so clean you could eat off its mud flaps, into which you can step to watch con-tinuously playing videos of idyllic country rides, or scrutinize an engine that's been sawn in two so you can see into the heart of "leg-endary German engineering." You exit the truck past mannequins posed like Samurai figures, dressed in fine leathers for BMW by Hein Gericke.

Local dealers, too, have set up shop, everything from Long

Island's Precision Leather's giant portable store purveying riding suits, jackets, pants, boots, raingear, and gloves of every possible thickness, weight, color, and price, to a little booth manned by the editor of a desktop-published free magazine covering the city cycle scene. Ghost Motorcycles, the Long Island source of my nostalgically remembered V50, has brought in a truckload of vintage and brand-new exotica, ancient Harleys with tasseled leather tractor-style seats and spanking new red Ducati superbikes. Young men with long tails of hair haul their girlfriends, in minuscule leather jackets and acid-washed jeans tucked into high-heeled boots that put them at a half run to keep up, past the European machines; they are bound for the Harley display and then the back of the hall. There the trials riding exhibition is about to start. They will crane their necks and press against other bodies piled deep around a cordoned-off oval a hundred feet wide to watch young teens defy gravity by standing on the pegs of their lightweight motocrossers and riding them up onto a trashed car's hood. Then up onto the roof, to pause as if frozen, finally to turn the machine 180 degrees around and ride back down. They speed up onto a ramp and fly off its end. They circle the ring entirely on the back wheel.

In 1994, the big thrill for a chosen few was the fact that for the first time in years, Moto Guzzi was making a formal appearance at the convention halls. Unlike the showing made by BMW's colorfully painted truck and full product line, including helmets, boots, motor oil, seven or eight models of bike, and anything else you can fit a logo on, the sum total of Guzzi's presence was two bikes, a standing sign smaller than a speed sign, and one director's chair for both the president of Moto America and his colleague, who also happened to be his wife. For some time, the Italian firm (at one point allied with Maserati) had had sales in the United States that would rival only those of a handicraft artist. A dealer who did ten units a year became a VIP. But from this valley Guzzi had started climbing the hill yet again, thanks to some finely crafted, expensive new sportbikes. Thanks is also due the perhaps bizarre but eminently sensible persistence of the Guzzi fanatic, who is not to be underestimated. Even if Guzzi were to stop sending any new machinery at all to these shores, there would still be Guzzis rumbling around the country into the next century, just enough for people to stop and ask, as they always have, "Say, what kind of bike is that?"

Carlo Guzzi once lived in a small town north of Lecco on the shore of Lake Como and rising into the mountains above it. Just prior to World War I, Guzzi had been concocting on paper motorcycle designs that he believed would eliminate the gaffes and ungainlinesses of contemporary two-wheeled vehicles. When he joined the fledgling but romantic ranks of the Italian air force, he met the two other men who he knew could help transform his ideas into salable metal: Giorgio Parodi, scion of a family of Genoan shipbuilders, and Giovanni Ravelli, an accomplished motorcycle racer. Together, he believed, they had all they would need to create a new breed. But within a few days of the war's end, when everything should have been starting, Ravelli died in a plane crash. The two remaining partners decided to commemorate the loss by taking the air force eagle as their logo.

Throughout the twenties, Guzzi machines made impressive showings on the racetracks of Italy and Europe, and after those occasions when they were shown up, Carlo Guzzi went back to the drawing table, or, rather, to a test engine he called his "mad machine," into which he could insert and test pistons and cylinders of any size. In 1928 they produced a model with a fully sprung frame (rear suspensions having proved heretofore difficult to master), which Carlo's brother Giuseppe took to the Arctic Circle on a proving run that gave it its nickname, Norge. Nineteen twenty-eight also saw the launch of what would become a long line of Motocarri—part bike, part truck. These joined an assortment of oddments also produced by the firm, including scooters, mopeds, and even a contraption whose front half was a motorcycle and whose rear was a tank with caterpillar treads. In various measure, they all helped bring the company through the inevitable lean times that might otherwise have put it under.

The Guzzi name was broadcast far wider than it had previously been by the spectacular wins in both Junior and Senior Manx TTs in 1935 with the Irishman Stanley Woods aboard. Woods had been a wise choice, hired because he knew the course in his sleep, unlike most Italian riders.

By 1934, Moto Guzzi was the preeminent motorcycle manufacturer in Italy, and its former small workshop in Mandello del Lario had expanded into a large factory employing seven hundred workers by digging into La Grigna, the mountain that rose sheerly from its premises. During the Second World War, the Mandello plant supplied the army with more than eight thousand Alce ("Elk") and Trialce (three-wheeled) cycles. Although Carlo Guzzi was notorious for looking jealously after every lira, in 1950 the company built what few other companies, motorcycle or otherwise, had: a full-scale wind tunnel ninety feet long, fitted with a 310-hp motor spinning a three-blade airscrew. (Once again, La Grigna's loss was Moto Guzzi's gain.) Its use allowed for the first time a scientific assessment—as opposed to an imaginative approximation—of how body design affected speed and handling. And that led, by 1954, to the creation of the first "dustbin" fairings for racing bikes, quickly borrowed by virtually all the other teams. These shells, which looked futurist and medieval at once, fully enclosed the front half of the bikes, leaving a few inches of tire to peep out from the bottom. What they helped riders to gain on the speed ledger was debited on that of safe cornering, however, and they were banned in 1957, the year that Moto Guzzi officially withdrew from racing.

This had the effect of simultaneously cutting short the life and canonizing the afterlife of an awesome machine then being created by the works racing division: a transverse V8. It developed a blunt 75 hp, which would have led it to flatten the competition if given the chance, but the major Italian firms, with the exception of the wealthy MV Agusta, had agreed that racing was beginning to empty the bank accounts faster than racing's marketing benefits were refilling them. They signed a pact and quit the scene. (By the time of their quitting, according to Mick Walker's *Italian Motorcycles*, the Mandello works had racked up the following: 14 World Championships; 134 world speed records; 47 Italian championships; 55 national titles; 11 Manx TTs; and a total of 3,327 international victories of all sorts.)

Giulio Cesare Carcano, an engineer with the firm since 1936 and now considered a genius by those who marvel at the ineffable beauties of a construction like the V8 racebike, did not survive the period of receivership in which the company found itself in the mid-sixties, after an industrywide crisis. Before he was shown the door, however, the dignified Carcano left Moto Guzzi with a small prize: a 90-degree V-twin design that for a short while was intended to soup up Fiat 500 cars. Instead, it ended up fulfilling the desires of the Polizia Stradale for a new mount. It became the V7, a 700cc twin with shaft drive.

The engine proved adaptable to the late-1960s American market as well, in large road-eater styles called the California, Eldorado, and Ambassador, many of which are still carrying their owners on long journeys through the countryside. Then designer Lino Tonti refined both engine and frame to unveil, in 1971, a stunning new machine: the V7 Sport. It was low and mean, handled like cream pours, and even standing still looked like something you could get on and *go*. A series of smaller twins based on the same engine layout, including the 500cc V50, was introduced in 1977.

In the States, in 1984, a former dentist began campaigning a Guzzi in endurance races as a privateer. His bike won the national championship, and repeated the next year. The V-twin design may not have been as up-to-date as the Japanese output, but the doctor had rightly appreciated its tenacious ability to take abuse. So he also figured he stood a chance in the speed contest then known as the Battle of the Twins (later Pro-Twins, then, predictably, Super Twins), which was created when twins became uncompetitive against four-cylinder engines.

John Wittner—known to all as Dr. John—is a very, very serious gearhead. He analyzed and machined and tested and mulled over and recast and retested new pieces for nearly every one of the hundreds on his racebike, draining his bank account in the process. He produced a new chassis, and tweaked the engine endlessly. Finally the last gremlins inside were subdued and the Guzzi won the twins series in 1987.

The results of this homegrown effort (which included many small contributions from the pockets of National Owners Club members) were not lost on the Italian headquarters. Now Dr. John, as pleasant and humble a man as one is likely to find in the echelons of truly driven, demented bike engineers, lives near the factory in the small Milanese resort town of Mandello del Lario, where his Italian continues to improve.

From the columns and letters of the *Moto Guzzi National Owners Club News:*

> I've commuted the sentence on at least two Guzzis and have my eyes on a '67 V700. I get a lot of bull from Harley riders at work until they ride the Eldorado and learn that I got 1¼ bikes for $500 while they spent 20 times that for a bike that's in the shop all the time. Of course I spent hundreds of hours working on the bike but I would probably do that with a new Harley if I had one. I'm not comfortable using something unless I know how it works. I guess in some way it's a sick sort of game with me. The Harley riders don't understand the pleasure I get from using parts from VWs, Fiats, and Kodak slide projectors on the bike. They've begun to call it Franken-Guzzi. In some ways I am playing god with it: I resurrected it and have made it in my own image and as I consider myself an individual so too is the bike totally unlike any other. [Peter Cushman, Worcester, Massachusetts]

> This brings us to the eccentric group of riders whose hearts belong to the machines from that little boot-shaped country in southern

Europe. I'm sure you've seen them lurking around, the dark, some-what oily chap wearing the same AGV leathers since Carter was President. The sort of fellow who will look right through the new ZX1100 just to get a glimpse of the ratty Lambretta scooter sitting behind it. The guy with the "Gas in my stomach, pasta in my tank" T-shirt who won't give a four-cylinder bike the time of day unless it says "Bimota" on the tank. [Nolan Woodbury, Coolidge, Arizona, "Roadworthy"]

I'm 65 years young—been riding since 1943—first bike was a 1928 Harley JD (wish I had it today). I've owned Indians, square fours, Vincents, just about every British motorcycle made. Was well into the Japanese makes when a friend who rode Moto Guzzi talked me into a temporary trade on one of our rides. Well, I had about given up on finding another bike that was as much fun to ride as those Triumphs and BSAs I rode back in the fifties—boy oh boy, how in heck could I have missed that Guzzi? I so enjoyed that ride I sold the Gold Wing I was riding and bought his Guzzi—even quit smoking so I'd last longer and get in a few more years and miles. [Forrest Waller, Jr., armed services overseas]

There are a few motorcycles whose mechanical design is naturally beautiful: the transverse four (or six . . . WOW) air-cooled engine with all the fine fins flying in the breeze and the graceful curved pipes like ram's horns flowing with the motion of the machine . . . the classic single, symmetrical by way of unity, standing like the mythic hero to lead the charge . . . and the horizontal twin, the textbook example of balance and cooling, as symmetrical as a mir-ror image. But the real beauty is the vee twin, with one cylinder reaching up and out from either side of the frame. The twin cylin-ders are positioned far enough forward that the visual mass is placed almost perfectly for an image of proficient handling. But I am a lover of machinery, its feels, its smell, the mettle of its metal . . . I love a grand aluminum casting, a sparkling machined surface, the perfect circle signature of a lathe, the perforated pattern of mill and drill. So the old Guzzi and I get along just fine. [Tom Chipley, Warrenton, Virginia, "The Existential Garage"]

Well, I did it, and am up to 501,000 miles on Moto Guzzis. So far I've never been left on the side of the highway broken down.

I was [once] riding with a hotrod Harley rider. He had a 74-cubic-inch. Pretty new Harley-Davidson. Anyway, he was riding in the lead, and I am on my 850 T-3 police bike. He was riding kinda fast, and then we came up to a stoplight and he yells, "Am I riding too fast for you?" After we got out on the open road again, I turned my T-3 on and passed him. After a little while I couldn't see him back there so I slowed down and stopped along the highway, waiting for him. When he came along side and stopped—I was laughing and said, "Was I going too fast for you?" He never forgot it and told his friends you can't fool around with Moto Guzzi, they're fast. [Charlie Pinheiro, Hendersonville, North Carolina, "Letters from Charlie"]

I remember one year in Ruidoso, New Mexico, Dan and Cynthia, his wife, rode up from Las Cruces to attend the Golden Aspen Motorcycle Rally. There were only about four Guzzis in attendance and Dan and Cynthia owned two of them. One Guzzi rider had some bad luck with a carburetor banjo and managed to break it beyond repair. Dan scavenged a banjo from Cynthia's bike. He decided he would make the run back to Las Cruces, a several hours' drive, for a replacement before the rally was over, saving a fellow Guzzi rider from a long delay waiting for parts to be shipped in. Bad luck runs in streaks and while the unfortunate Guzzi owner was trying to complete repairs, he managed to break the new part also. Dan didn't get upset, he simply pulled off a new banjo and installed it himself. He then rode all the way back home to get spare parts to put Cynthia's bike back in running order. [Dave Shultz, Ruidoso, New Mexico]

Except for letters from my kids, the "News" is about all I look forward to seeing in my mailbox. [A. R. Newman, Port Hadlock, Washington]

January 2nd only comes around once a year, thank goodness. This year, 1995, marks my 46th birthday, by itself no great feat, but it was also the day that I embarked on my 30th birthday ride! I began this tradition in Cleveland, Ohio, with a ride on my brother's Vespa. He was in Korea and graciously left it behind. I assumed it was mine to ride and simply told my folks that this was Jim's gift to me. I don't know why they believed me but they did. So I threw a leg over the ugly thing and rode until my fingers were nearly frostbit. It was a personal celebration.

Over the years I rode BMWs, BSAs, Triumphs, Harleys, Suzukis, and Hondas of my own, plus friends' Yamahas, Harleys, and Kawasakis when mine weren't running or in those lean years when I didn't own a bike (never again). They were rides in the rain, snow, slush, and sleet as well as beautifully sunny days. The temperatures ranged from very close to 0 all the way to the 60s. I've been healthy as a horse and ready to go and seen the other side of that coin, too. In 1987 I took my birthday ride on my R65 Beemer only a few short weeks after being released from the hospital for open heart surgery. That was definitely the most painful ride of the bunch but also the most inspiring. I knew I was alive and had never been so happy about it! My birthday rides have been as short as around the block (during a blizzard where you couldn't see ten feet in front of you) to several hundred miles in the northern snow-covered mountains of Iran where it was very cold, slippery, and scary.

As the sticker on the back of my helmet says, "Motorcycles saved my life." Again and again! [Ray Hale, Gainesville, Florida]

As soon as the airplane starts down the runway, with the powerful buildup of speed that presses one into the back of the seat and that for me accurately mimics the inexorability with which I believe the final conflagration is approaching, I switch on my Walkman. It plays tape one of Glenn Gould's performance of Bach's *Goldberg Variations*. The recording engineers have not been able to completely erase the sound of Gould's intake of breath and impulsive humming behind the insistence of the piano, and it is this ragged human breath that keeps the airplane up.

Also, in this case, the fact that I had Luc's hand to squeeze into whiteness. Thus we would not be going down over the black Atlantic, although I had no real way to know that. And so I sat there through the night in the narrow seat while around me everyone napped under blue KLM blankets. Although I was exhausted from not sleeping much for the past week, the whole night through I was kept awake by being about three seconds away from the fullest outward expression of severe nausea. Like a mantra I kept repeating to myself: "There is a bag. You can use it if you need to. There is a bag." But my anxiety would not be so kind as to spend itself in such a déclassé way. Nor could the stewardess provide mint tea or Maalox. So for seven hours I sat transfixed by sickness.

Then we landed in Amsterdam. The prop-hop to Brussels was curiously, suddenly fun, during which I felt the absence of all fear and only pleasurable anticipation. Then we were driven south to Liège, to an old city in ancient Wallonia where we would spend the next few months. I was armed only with a duffel stuffed with riding gear and with the phone numbers of the American representative of the Moto Guzzi National Owners Club in Germany, David Smith, and a Dutch enthusiast of old Guzzi singles named Ivar de Gier. I was planning to buy a bike and ride around Europe for a couple of months while my husband researched a book about the country of his birth. But I had no real idea what I was getting into; I kept trying to remind myself this was the true essence of travel.

(I marvel that at some point when I wasn't looking, something transformed me from the kid who can hardly wait to get onto the roller coaster into the person who frets constantly that it may fragment into splinters at any moment. Jeesh.)

I could not imagine going to the birthplace of motorcycles, or being within hailing distance of Mandello del Lario, my version of Lourdes, without riding, although I was not able to foot the price of a rental or the fee to transport my own motorcycle overseas. So I took a flying leap into irresponsibility, trusting to the mercy of strangers and to the hope that if I purchased a machine I could keep it upright and unstolen long enough to sell it back before I left.

Under what circumstances could you send off a letter to some previously unknown person in a town in Holland you can't find on a map and enter into a correspondence in which the initial investment of one page and a forty-five-cent stamp is returned in replies of six pages and more (neatly typed in nearly perfect English, from a respondent who turns out to speak ten or eleven languages, including Gaelic), culminating in an offer to take the writer to a Dutch dealer, vouch for her riding ability though he knows nothing of it, and put her up while the transaction is conducted—at his parents', if moral comfort is a question?

There may be others that I am not aware of, but in this case the circumstances were simply that I had come across Ivar de Gier's name in an issue of the Guzzi club news. But it was David Smith who was to top even de Gier's generosity.

Luc and I settled in the Liège Holiday Inn, of all places, for what we thought would be a night or two but turned into the longest week of our lives while we waited, and waited, for our apartment to be vacated by the previous tenants. For the first couple of days I wandered around town with increasing trepidation about my upcoming European riding debut: I watched how the small cars zipped along the avenues, managed to stop somehow when pedestrians stepped suddenly into crosswalks, and continuously merged and combined with other lines of traffic that included zinging scooters, two-strokes, buses, bicycles, all flowing, flowing, ceaselessly. Roads curved, then melted away; mysterious signs punctuated the junctions, and two-way streets were marked with the white-dotted lines that to me had always signified multilane one-ways. I saw many motorcycles on the roads, but never parked anywhere. Where did they all go? And where was I going to put mine when I got it?

No matter how much I worried, I had set things in motion and, in ideal form for me, I had forced myself into a place where I would just have to figure it out as I went along. I weighed both offers of help, and I decided to go with David Smith's over Ivar de Gier's. Smith would come from Germany at the end of the week to pick me up and take me back to check out a bike he had located for sale near his home.

I walked into the dark bar lounge in the Holiday Inn and stopped for a moment to let my eyes adjust to the light. A couple dozen men were sitting about, but only one of them could possibly be David Smith: the one in the Guzzi suspenders, leather vest bearing a pewter pin in the shape of an Ambassador's engine block, and black leather pants tucked into knee-high boots with a green-white-and-red-striped cutaway crest the size of a butter plate over each shin.

After twenty-seven years working for the U.S. military in personnel, on assignment in Germany, Vietnam, Saudi Arabia, and Germany again, Smith was settling into retirement when he was still young enough to properly enjoy it. His salt-and-pepper hair had been allowed to grow after decades of regulation tight rein and now brushed his shoulders when it was not pulled back. A mustache joined a triangle of brushy beard, and all in all he not distantly resembled Custer.

Smith lives in a small hamlet near Ramstein Air Base, in a third-floor apartment he shares with his German wife, who remains a shoe saleswoman in the department store serving the base. The office in his apartment is the headquarters of the European branch of the Moto Guzzi National Owners Club, and although Belgium, Holland, England, Italy, Luxembourg, France, and Germany are not yet one nation, the members from these countries rather like the misleading title of their club. The honorary membership card on which he typed my name, number 295, bears the motto "We stand united to help fellow Guzzi riders." As the president, or rather the king, of the European division, Smith is a supreme role model. He had ridden for nearly four hours to get to the Holiday Inn. The next morning we would wake at five-thirty in the morning, eat the bread and cheese he had thought to bring for both of us while standing in the dark in the hotel's parking lot, ride fast back to Germany on his SPIII (a new 1000cc touring model), go test-ride the Guzzi 650 he had thought a likely candidate for me, then return to his home, exchange the SP for his car, and drive back to Belgium, whereupon he would decline the offer of a bed and turn around again for Germany— somewhere around 750 miles in one day, amazing to me but not unusual for a man who turned out to have a serious high-mileage jones. He would expect nothing in return for this round robin except that I find a nice bike to enjoy while I was in Europe.

There is nothing like the first time. And since that is so, we all keep looking for new firsts. When things feel new, it is as if you have been given back your eyes, your sense of smell. In a foreign country, buying butter at the market is a marvelous adventure, discovering how the coin-op laundry works is a wonderment. Here, I study new protocols. Certain types of beer demand certain accompaniments, like a tiny bowl of cheese cubes doused in celery salt, or miniature pretzels. Coffee always comes with a cookie or piece of chocolate on the saucer. The refrigerator in our apartment overlooking the Meuse River and its barges has its own peculiar cycle, every half hour or so emitting a vague sound into the room that sounds exactly like a spaceship coming in for a soft landing in a sci-fi movie from the fifties.

I had ridden motorcycles innumerable times on highways before, but in Europe I did it again for the first time. The German countryside would look similar enough to a combination of Vermont and

Ohio to lull me for a while, then something would cause a voice I did not recognize as my own to say in my head, "You are in *Germany*," and a shiver would run through me.

I had gotten a wad of cash, packed up my biking gear, and taken a convoluted series of trains to get back to Kaiserslautern, where David picked me up at the station. We had planned to go to the base to change the money, spend the night at his apartment, and use the next day to pick up the V65 and register and insure it. But when I arrived, David's face looked dark. He informed me his wife had somehow gotten the idea that we were having an affair. She would not allow me in the house. He apologized, a bit more upset than I was, and wheeled the car around to look for suitable lodgings for me.

He did the talking at the inn, as I had not prepared myself sufficiently for doing business in Germany by learning German. I was to regret this fact more than I could have imagined, never more so than the next day, when I got lost in a rainstorm, stopped in a small town, and attempted to get directions, or even a passerby to look my way, using the only German word I could come up with, from a head filled with old World War II movies: *Bitte, bitte . . .*

So. It was early evening. I was in Kaiserslautern with my own two feet and little else.

I walked down one sidewalk until the town ended, then walked back up the other. No one was about. I who avoided most human connection when it was possible now became desperate for it, when it was not. I began to look for a phone. There were many machines vending nuts and gum posted several times along each block, but no phones. I grew excited when I spied a red booth up ahead, and I ran toward it. Strangely, it was sitting on someone's lawn. Then I realized it was a denatured English phone booth, acting as garden statuary.

In the vestibule of the hostel there was no phone, but there was a cigarette vending machine, so I spent $3.75 on a pack and called it dinner. I slowly climbed the creaky steps to my narrow room, which contained a swaybacked bed and a sink. I lay down to read the copy of *Stars and Stripes* I had cadged from David, since I had neglected to bring any reading material. That took me all of ten minutes. Then I took out my travel diary and wrote. I took an Advil. I looked at my watch. I wondered how in hell I was going to sleep. I listened to the mysterious sounds coming through the thin walls: thuddings and lockings and unlockings, footsteps up, footsteps down, footsteps pausing, more unlockings and lockings. I slept at last, waking through the night to thuddings and muffled laughter. This was where the base's servicemen came to spend the night with their women.

There is nothing on earth quite like German bureaucracy. The functionary to whom David appealed with my application to register a vehicle to be taken out of the country did everything in her power to resist, showing us aggressively disconsolate little smiles over the protestations of her boss in the next cubicle, who was equally determined we should have the papers. The whole process would take many hours, and many journeys back and forth from other rooms and other buildings, to placate the various fickle spirits who rule the state regulatory agencies. I was informed I must leave Germany with the bike that day and never return with it.

David escorted me a few miles onto the highway. As he exited and I sped past his waving figure, a funny admixture of trepidation and exhilaration gathered in me, as if I were standing at the top of a black-diamond ski run with my blue-square skills. At the very least, I was about to get my habit of making safe, smooth lane changes and always being aware of the traffic both ahead and behind me shot quickly to hell on the autobahn. I had decided to baby the engine of this 1984 V65 (essentially a bumped-up V50) so I could rescue as much money from it as possible when it came time to sell, and I thought 75 mph a decent cruising speed for it. I would check my rearview and see nothing whatsoever behind. Then, eyes back at the fore, a second or two later there would be a Mercedes blur to my left. Just as quickly it would disappear off ahead.

Overhead it was charcoal gray. To the northwest, exactly in my path, streaks of sky seeped toward earth. After I turned off the highway onto a two-lane road with a Saab trying to kiss my rear wheel and a truck slowing down ahead, I rode directly under a sky that looked like dirty cotton batting. Lightning sheared a ragged white line through it, quickly followed by a loud crack that reverberated over the fields to my left. My face shield grew dots that refracted the light; they multiplied into an opaque film. Now I could feel them on my gloves, and suddenly they began stinging me through the leather. The road ahead looked textured. The peppering smacks against my body, I suddenly realized, were not raindrops but hail. I would have stopped had there been a shoulder, or slowed had there not been the insistent Saab. But I had no choice but to ride on at a pace not my own, and thus no use for speculation as to what I should do if the ice accumulated over the pavement. There is nothing like the first time.

There has never been the profound need for things to be big in Europe as there is in the United States. America's lumberingly over-sized cars have usually been explained as a response to the comparatively enormous distances they were required to cover as well as to our lock on sizable oil reserves. Indeed, with a full tank costing some sixty dollars in Europe, autos there could more cheaply run on red wine. But it occurs to me that another piece of what causes cars to stay small in Europe—and keeps motorcycles in a privileged place—is a desire to go places not only fast, but sinuously fast. Watch the traffic in most European cities; look at the design of some Italian or German cars. They don't want to cruise, they want to go. And they don't want to pose, unless it's to give a tantalizing glimpse at 170 km/h. Idling your car is not the pastime it is in the United States, and there are fewer traffic jams in moderate-size cities simply because it doesn't take a car five turns and the whole roadway to back into a parking space. You can pay for the chance to run your vehicle on the Nürburgring track, and everyone does it: cars, motorbikes, even buses and delivery trucks. "Those crazy Germans," a Belgian says. "Every weekend there someone gets killed."

Let's face it: I have eyes for Italian motorcycles largely, but not only, because my first motorcycle was an Italian motorcycle. In the same way, because my dog is a Border collie, I love Border collies, am enthralled by Border collies and their behavioral tics, would go out of my way to watch Border collies do their thing. I have become a connoisseur of Border collies, and though the qualities I admire so faithfully in them are real and objective, I have no doubt that if the puppy who came out of the cage at the shelter and into our lives had grown up to be a Labrador retriever, I would extoll at length the many virtues of Labs.

Since I come from a family that found anything more technical than changing light bulbs a job for experts, my love of motorcycles is not mainly based on the engineering miracles that send others into raptures. And although I feel a fascination born of both envy and the exotic appeal of foreignness for those mechanically oriented souls who are fearless in the face of exploded diagrams and who have obviously divined the mysteries of tools, always in possession of the proper implement for any job (and where is the Susan Sontag who will write an erotics of highly specialized equipment?), my kind of admiration starts from outside.

Thus, to me, some of today's Japanese crotch rockets look a bit too much like Mighty Morphin Power Rangers to command high aesthetic respect, not to mention the fact that they call up in me the vestiges of a vague childhood fear of toy robots. The genesis of their design can be traced back to *Astro Boy;* the mammoth tanks over which riders stretch like figures clinging to missiles, the impossibly wide rear tires, the squashed, biomorphic tails remind me of a sight from which I always recoil—the overpumped, steroidal practitioners of obsessive bodybuilding. But they are a hell of a lot of fun to ride.

In Italian machines I see what I consider the manifestation of national traits, like extravagant sensuality, dunderheaded stubbornness, and an affection for the pure sex of line. They spring from the same occult source, after all, as an unfairly large share of the world's most exquisite stuff: architecture, sculpture, drawing, food, furniture, fashion design. So Italy has also institutionalized cheating and graft on a grand scale—who wants perfection?

And that is exactly what the proponents of Moto Guzzis like so much about them. "They have character," they always say; a short-hand for "cantankerous," sure, but if that were all, Guzzis would be rusting in barns and not plying the roads twenty and thirty years after their births. They are like us—receptive to extraordinary improvements but never made perfect; full of torque and rumble; requiring a fair amount of care but always returning the investment in full. If a motorcycle is just a vehicle on which to get someplace, Guzzis are not motorcycles.

Guzzis appeal to the middle-class rider who is not too racy, but plenty individualistic. Their many quirks ensure that everybody will need somebody else sometime, and the relatively few numbers they attract ensure that everybody will be somebody sometime. Their riders are oriented toward touring, and by "touring" read "zillions of miles." They attract tinkerers, people for whom good enough is never good enough, for whom the rituals of necessary maintenance are secret joys, and for whom a professional mechanic is a figure out of a storybook. Never for them a full fairing that would hide, as if it were somehow distasteful, the innards that are their outsides, the motors that are their true meaning and beauty and the badge of their heritage. They allow their owners the fierce pride of being different, onto which these people hold ever more tightly as the world is overtaken by increasing waves of conformity.

"Power age economy has substituted the specialized machine and the assembly line for the craftsman, and has transformed many a skilled worker into a machine tender, with a resulting concentration, not upon excellence, but upon volume of product. The average city worker is asked to accept a wage or salary as a substitute for pride in workmanship and the satisfaction of mastery over tools and materials." These words, from *Living the Good Life*, published in 1954, explain some of the rationale behind Helen and Scott Nearing's successful experiment in living a self-sufficient life in which they produced their own food and shelter using largely their own hands. But it just as perfectly explains why people love such motorcycles as Moto Guzzis; they are a cure for what ails us, or for what alienates us from our own abilities. They call for the individual to achieve mastery over tools and materials, even as they are themselves tools with which we can repair the feeling that we have all become machine tenders of one sort or another.

And there are few things that exemplify pride of craftsmanship like a motorcycle that has been so modified by the owner, according to taste and wish, that it becomes effectively a one-off. On these exceptional bikes there is not a bolt or a hose or a gear that has not been reconsidered, replaced, rebuilt. Some of this extravagant attention is explained by the fact that, unlike the equally time-lavished gardening or hand-knitting project, the owner will entrust his or her life to the resulting creation. But safety in no measure really accounts for the impulse to remake motorcycles. Perhaps the next gene discovered by those scientists whose mandate seems to be smoothing worries by finding simple, preordained explanations for every sticky thing will be the one for the human need to make things with our own hands. As the necessity to do so in daily life continues to decline in the western world, motorcycles will provide for their owners a greater share of the fulfilled calm that comes only from experiencing handwork's full circuit of trial and error, aspiration and achievement.

As I found by sheer happenstance, when you buy a Moto Guzzi, you don't just buy a machine that goes fast, looks handsome, and has a one-year warranty on parts and labor. You buy a thousand friends.

Every owner of a Moto Guzzi in Europe knows the way to Mandello del Lario by heart. David Smith goes several times a year, although it can't always be to procure parts, even if he does keep a stable of needy older models in the United States to ride on visits home. Since he had just been there the week before I wanted to go, however, even he had to decline the opportunity for another trip of several hundred miles. He gave me the name of the acting head of the Moto Guzzi Club Belgium instead, and I rode north toward Antwerp one day to go on a club run with them and to meet Luc Van Vossel.

Luc VV—appropriately enough, "V-twin," but I will call him "the second"—is, in his words, "a simple office clerk" for the Belgian railway. He never finished university, although he is thoroughly fluent in Dutch, French, and English. His modest salary pays for a modest apartment and a few record albums every now and again, and all the rest goes to satisfy the Guzzi gods. He attends rallies all over Europe whenever the supply of francs allows, and he says he is a member of that inner circle for whom "Moto Guzzi is more than just that bike in the garage. It occupies most of our free time. We even travel a thousand kilometers [over six hundred miles] in one day to go to a bike meet and ride back those thousand kilometers two days later."

Luc II, an imp with buzzed blond hair, rapid-fire laugh, avid taste for good wine, and teeth that are in need of professional attention, led a group of thirty or so motorcycles on a fifty-mile route he had been carefully planning since one icy day in winter. Now we painted a motorcyclist's Millet, snaking through the misty green Flemish landscape past canal and windmill, ancient stone barn and grazing horse. No one broke rank; no one tested the sidewalls of tires. We kept to a genteel speed, and up ahead I saw the turn signals of twelve motorcycles winking in unison, while in my rearview I could see the headlights of many more. There were cruiser-style Californias ridden two-up; a couple of sidecar rigs; fathers with children on the back. We had eaten breakfast together before the ride, and I had chatted with a young woman named Ines who was riding pillion on her husband's BMW K1 (he also owned a Guzzi); she had left her Kawasaki 750cc Zephyr at home, as well as their baby. She told me how she had ridden until her second trimester, when she quit without reflection, thinking as a matter of course it would be permanent. Then, when her baby was several months old, it came to her as a fully formed thought: Having babies could not be analogous to giving up life. And since a significant part of her life, a joyous part, had been taken up with riding motorcycles, she decided she owed it to herself, and by extension her child, to continue. Her parents were happy to baby-sit. She was now thinking about getting a sidecar, a popular option for young families in Europe. Baby seats fit perfectly in sidecars.

After the ride we all stopped for coffee, taking over an entire café. There Luc II told me he would be happy to escort me to Mandello. If he rode south to Liège and spent the night with us, we could leave early enough to ride from Belgium through Luxembourg (we'll make sure to buy gas there, he informed me; it's much cheaper), France, Germany (to hell with the restriction on my bike's papers), Switzerland, and northern Italy, making it to Lake Como that night.

My alarm rang at 5:00 a.m., and I was quiet as I moved toward the kitchen so as to give Luc II, asleep on the living-room couch, a half hour more. I put on water for coffee, glanced outside from five floors up at a barge moving its dark weight of raw material silently down the Meuse, then went into the bathroom. In the white expanse of the bathtub there was a spider climbing the slick side, tumbling down, then starting its Sisyphean ascent once more. In addition to the fact that I take no being's life without damn good cause, loath even though I am to share my toilette with arachnids, I am particularly sensitive to portents, and killing spiders is one of the more serious. Especially before a ride, all talismans must be ordered: my watch on my right wrist, my mother's gold 1952 class ring given me upon my graduation from the same college on my right little finger, the same tube of lipstick and crumpled dollar bill always zipped into the pocket of my jacket. There is no god who guides the universe, alas, so I know this is useless, but it has worked so far. And what is not broken should not be fixed, or even breathed on.

I carefully picked up the spider and deposited him behind the radiator. I turned on the spigots for a bath and hurried into the kitchen to catch the whistling kettle. The coffee was filtering as I returned to the bathroom, where the spider lay in need of last rites on the surface of the bathwater.

Within an hour we were walking toward my garage, where Luc had parked his brand-new, shiny red 1000cc Le Mans next to my V65. As I opened the door, I peered into the underground darkness and could see that something was not as we had left it the night before. Look, Luc, I said, someone's moved your bike.

Indeed someone had. Run into it with a car, then picked it up and left a note in French on the seat. "Your bike was badly placed and I couldn't maneuver my car. It fell down. Sorry."

The Le Mans had gone down on its right side. The spark-plug cap was smashed, along with the end of the plug. The turn signal was pulverized.

We had estimated our riding day at thirteen hours, but it was now going to be a very pushed-back thirteen hours. There was nothing to be done but wait for a shop to open to get a new cap and plug; the turn signal could be taped together for a later fix.

Luc was gallant, saying it could have been worse, which it always could be, but he was angry and dismayed beneath his manners. Although he was an avowed pacifist, he would have made an exception for this guy.

Nine o'clock found us at the local Italian bike mechanic's to pick up parts, which took but a few minutes to install when we returned. In the meanwhile we had lost four hours. In atonement for this happening on my watch, in my garage, I neglected to replace my gas cap when filling up before we finally left and had to buy another in Switzerland.

We had ridden together on the V65 to the same mechanic I had consulted previously on the matter of a few mysterious stall-outs; he had done some work and pronounced the patient cured. So I was not pleased when the engine now died at a couple of stoplights on the way over, proving difficult to start up again. But I was so insistent upon going to Italy—and nothing steels my resolve like an ominous progression of actual problems, in direct contrast to imaginary ones—I did not want to entertain the idea of postponing. A few hours later, at a Lorraine toll booth, the bike quit again, and this time the ignition provided only a sad clicking down in the starter. Under an aggressive sun we peeled off all the luggage to look at every electrical connection accessible to the naked eye. But neither Luc nor I would score high on a mechanic's test. He suggested we bump-start the bike. "Put it in second gear, and when I've pushed you fast enough to say when, let out the clutch." No problem, I thought: I've done this plenty of times, and besides, I've got the easy part. Luc applied all his sweaty force to the back of the seat. Fire away!

But it happened again in Germany. And a few more times when I was able to restart it with the ignition. Then came Switzerland.

Inside the St. Gotthard tunnel, a 23-km sweatbox of carbon monoxide and dull yellow light, I looked down at the instrument panel. The battery light was gently glowing, a probable sign the battery was not completely recharging. This is not comforting information when you still have twenty minutes of riding left in something that offers as much emergency egress as a slot-car track.

It was late in the day and we had already passed through a couple of showers, storms that appeared suddenly on exiting a tunnel that had been entered in sunshine. But we had been making good time. It was looking more and more possible that we might make Lake Como in one day after all.

The Swiss follow speed limits, since the gendarmes not only clock them with the *dernier cri* in radar but line them up and demand cash on the spot. So we were not compelled to race our engines or anyone else. I watched as the Alps revealed themselves like an accordion-fold postcard set, and I smiled behind the helmet: Here I am, and this is real.

The next moment I felt the power drop off, even more suddenly than when the tank runs dry. I reflexively closed the throttle and then opened it right up again, and the engine came to life. It was the most bizarre feeling, like losing and recovering your balance on a beam so fleetingly that no memory of that awful tremble underfoot can be retained.

Now it was growing colder, cold seeping in everywhere and nothing to stop it. The sun had decamped behind the mountains, and with its going the Kodachrome surroundings were transformed into the echoing gray insides of a great Frigidaire, the air cooled by means of those banks of white ice forever flowing down the crests around us.

When it happened the next time, the engine would not rekindle itself. The lights on the little panel all blinked on to signal total refusal as I glided to a stop by the side of the highway. But before a full stop I hit the starter button. She fired up, so we were on our way. Until a few kilometers later, when it happened once more. Then again and again and again at unpredictable intervals. My body was involuntarily and unstoppably trembling with cold and anxiety. When we stopped for gas along the now lonely highway, Luc coaxed me on by saying the border was just a few miles away; indeed, the woman who took our money spoke Italian, not German. In another hour and a half we could be in Mandello.

It was ten o'clock, dark and frigid. Luc phoned ahead to a European division friend of his in Mandello and told him to put the coffee on.

Did the V65 smell the place of its birth? How else to explain the fact that every time it died, it would resurrect itself, albeit now with a loud protest of backfires? As we passed through the city of Lecco on the eastern fork of the lake, the bike was reenacting the Easter miracle every kilometer or so. At one point it coasted toward a stop right next to a pair of carabinieri, who looked prepared to ask a serious question or two. But as long as we were still coasting, a brutal twist of the wrist might do the trick. This time it fired up with a double explosion from the pipes. The police jumped back, and we continued on.

When my headlight finally found what it was looking for and I saw ahead a sign saying MANDELLO, I felt almost as if I had made it to the crest of the Matterhorn on crutches.

Luc led the way to his friend Paolo's apartment house. We were in

Italy, all right, in the middle of an Italian Neorealist movie. From every apartment the sound of heavy-bosomed mothers berating wayward husbands and daughters echoed through the wide stairwell lit by a single bulb. Inside, Paolo had not only made some thick coffee, he had also reheated some chicken noodle soup. He and Luc conversed in a version of French to which my high school language skills did not permit me full entrance, so I smiled a lot. Luc bent his head toward me and whispered that I really must have some of the soup Paolo offered with such obvious pride. After nearly twenty meatless years, smilingly swallowing this soup was a challenge of the highest order. It was made much more so by the fact that something in the soup had gone bad. Luc grimaced only once when Paolo wasn't looking, but he finished his bowl in a trice. His friend was well pleased, refilling it immediately.

At much past midnight we set out for our hotel, Paolo leading the way. The taillight of his California was the only thing I saw, or could see. I had entered another state of consciousness, one in which I did things but did not feel any of them. We were obviously winding through the streets of Mandello, then we were climbing. Up and up, a hairpin or two, then up once more. At last we were going down a bit that seemed even steeper than what we had climbed, and then we were at the door of the Al Verde Inn. In the morning there was the side of a misty green mountain backed up against the window, and I had to step out onto the balcony to be able to see its peak, just below which was a little wooden shepherd's hut with smoke curling out of the chimney pipe. This was too bloody picturesque for words.

The scenery out the front door of the inn only made me stop in astonishment: I rode a motorcycle down *that*? The driveway was so steep that it would be possible to ride back up it only if you did not pause.

We spent two days in the town, eating pizza and trying to spy past electric gates at hillside villas of gorgeously weathered stucco. At the official Guzzi dealer in town, Agostini, a large and sophisticated affair, we talked at length with the owner's daughter. Wearing a camel-colored cashmere twin sweater set and a strand of pearls, she kept running her hand through her creamy blond hair as she addressed the subject of why motorcycles are always female. You could tell hers were, at any rate.

David Smith had left a little present for me on his visit the previous week: the phone number of John Wittner—Dr. John—and some kind of story he'd given them at the factory that I was a dignitary deserving special treatment. Luc could barely contain his glee as we were thus escorted on a factory tour by an Italian-speaking muckety-muck who did not check our credentials, and we looked agape at the famous wind tunnel and the museum containing "the most representative models which have been acknowledged as internationally important in the motorcycle evolution" and acres of V-twin engines awaiting assembly and Californias being loaded onto trucks and a Quota dual-purpose being smacked through its gears on the dyno. We were told the factory now produces about 5,500 machines a year, though it can and has made 35,000. Then we were guided into a high-ceilinged, fluorescent-lit reception room—shades of de Sica again—and after a short wait in came Dr. John. Hi, how ya doin'? The guy smiles all the time; he is energetic and wiry and for some reason put me in mind of an anthropomorphized grasshopper out of the *Fables* of La Fontaine. We went and had a pasta lunch that was so leisurely you'd think he didn't have Big Responsibilities pressing on him like lead plates, and he told us all sorts of secrets about what was going on inside the company even if they weren't secrets at all.

The V65 had spent the day with the man reputed to be Mandello's most remarkable electrical wizard, and indeed I felt as though we had come to that point in the movie when the Tin Man is buffed by giant rollers and the Cowardly Lion gets his mane done up in powder and bows. The bike was pronounced, with a wide smile and a sweep of the arm, definitively cured.

And it was, until we got to Switzerland again. The definitive breakdown occurred, with rare foresight, near Trimbach, within pushing distance of the parking lot of a restaurant wherein worked a young waitress who loved New York and wanted very much to visit Manhattan and would love to hear something about it. That secured the bike for the night, and as I waited for Luc to return from a hotel-reconnaissance mission I stared at the cows across the road wearing red-felt-lined leather collars from which hung sonorous brass bells. I had thought that was just another thing they trotted out for tourists, but then I was learning so much on this trip.

Let it not be said motorcycles have no conscience. The highway exit where the V65 had breathed her last was about fifteen minutes from the facilities of Otto von Arx, Switzerland's Guzzi importer. There, in a warehouse-size shop that was so clean and orderly it was creepy, the Italian-born mechanic went methodically over every inch of wire in the vehicle until he found the small but guilty corroded contact. I had told Luc to head home without me, as he was about to miss a day of work on my account. "We have a saying in my club," he intoned. "'Ride out together, ride home together.'" And so it was to be. Besides, as I later learned, Luc too was under the misapprehension that I had powers I did not have. He was hoping I would write something about him and that the words would exude a fragrance attractive to a nice girl, one who could break a run of bad luck in which he fell in love with women who over time revealed themselves to be rather lunatic. On this trip, he earned more than one nice girl. I only wished I could produce them for him.

Motorcycles are a way in to yourself, and a way out. For those who work on them, they provide a simulacrum of life itself—the project that is finished only when you are. The improvements they can stand are limited only by the amount of ingenuity you can spare, the time, the focus, the willingness to examine, tear down, think and rethink. But they are comforting in a way life cannot be, for, in their role as surrogate bodies, they may become sick, yet they can always get well.

People talk about a machine-age aesthetic, but machines are not considered beautiful so much for their own qualities as for their resemblance to us. As with our gods, we have never been able to conceive of much that does not take after ourselves. The organic appeal of the machine, however, has a twist: the possibility of rational perfectibility. What human would not wish to project himself upon such a form?

My persistent unconscious belief that every moment is a catastrophe waiting to happen was easily displaced onto the body of my motorcycle. And when I saw this perverse idea take shape outside me I could see it at last. It seemed to me to deliver a challenge, inviting me to meet it for battle on the ground of a white motorcycle.

Apparently, I was not the only person whose secret life was so shameful, so cowardly. Fear like mine was so common it had given rise to a virtual industry. The library's shelves were filled with dozens and dozens of books aimed at the reader who suffers fears she or he can not contain, fears that shred life. In these books I found the compilation of symptoms that allowed me a diagnosis: panic disorder. In it, the body's adrenaline fuel injection system is triggered by the mind. But it malfunctions, sticking open. You are caught forever in the moment when you first see the gun held against your neck.

I read about obsessive-compulsive disorder, too, and found it might as well be the same thing. The repetitive hand-washer or door-checker fears germs or intruders, just as the panicked fear heart attacks or losing control or cancer; all are agents of some unimaginable disaster. And always, the spiral of terror has its origin in the self's terrible demand that it must control that which cannot be controlled: every minute of one's fate.

The books were pretty helpful, if only for the queer comfort of reading case history after case history of people who described feeling exactly as I did. They too had felt that at every moment death was at hand. And if they were still alive to tell the tale, what were the chances I alone would perish?

The way out of yourself that motorcycles provide is toward life. In the words of Antoine de Saint-Exupéry, "When we exchange manly handshakes, compete in races, join together to save one of us who is in trouble, cry aloud for help in the hour of danger—only then do we learn that we are not alone on earth."

A Swiss friend told me the sad story of his well-to-do family. His autocratic father succeeded in driving his mother to a breakdown, after which she was pacified to incapacity by drugs. Confined to bed and half-hallucinatory, she began to rail against the man who had helped put her there. "Your needs—it's always *your* needs. What about mine? *I* need to get on a big motorbike and ride to Zurich!"

### ACTUAL DREAM, NIGHT OF JULY 30, 1995

For some reason, I am apparently still living at home with my parents. The next thing I know, I am in this weird, flat, sunny suburbia of square blocks and evenly placed houses. Where am I? I hear my mother's voice say we have moved to Indianapolis. What? We've moved? Why didn't you tell us, give us some warning, so we could say goodbye and cut our ties? As the implications of the news sink in, I start to think of all I have left behind and will never see again. I begin to cry, then to sob. I need help, so I phone a therapist whose name I'd found in the Indianapolis yellow pages, and he is extremely rude to me. My crying redoubles; I stand on the street lost, alone. Somebody passing by spits out at me with disgust, "Why don't you get yourself a therapist?" I protest that I have a perfectly good one at home, who helped me and was kind, whom I will never see again. [I am actually crying in my sleep by now.] Then I get a sudden thought, and the sadness lifts like magic: But maybe they have a good Moto Guzzi shop here!

Within a week of arriving home from my months in Europe, I was heading to New Hampshire once more. I did not feel as excited about the prospect as I used to, and I began to think that perhaps this particular wad of gum had lost its flavor. Maybe it was time to break out the maps again.

As I rode into New England in the usual heat, I began to ride into memories of Europe. They flashed past like mile markers on the side of the road. I was happy to have the Lario back under me—we fit each other. But even though it had given me hell, I mourned the V65 for a moment. I recalled the day its new owner, a professor at Delft Technical University, came to pick it up. After lunch in our Liège kitchen—Tom de Wilde and his wife had been laying bets all the way down from Holland, they told us while eating the salad, bread, cheese, and fruit we had laid out, on what kind of fatty, processed meat Americans would serve—Tom rode away on the Guzzi following his wife's car. I had felt a pang. I had gone back upstairs to sit on the couch until the last imagined echo of my former motorcycle disappeared down the streets. Across the Meuse, bikes had wailed back and forth on the highway along the riverside. It had been a recriminatory sound to me.

Now I recalled the day when, in Germany again, a multinational group of us (a German, a Swiss, a Belgian, an American, and a couple from Milton Keynes, England) had stopped off at a motorcycle museum in a little town called Otterbach. We admired all the fine old bikes, from Aermacchi to Zündapp, sure, but I think we were at least as appreciative of the fact that they were housed in a former church. It was still a house of worship as far as we were concerned.

Then I thought about my first ride in a sidecar, graciously offered by a young, modish Dutchman at a Guzzi rally, also in Germany. The car these days was usually reserved for his rosy, round baby, the pillion seat for his pretty wife; he scoffed at the idea that they would have quit riding after the baby came, since, after all, they had gotten married on the bike. For the duration of the poker run, though, I got to enjoy a sensation not unlike being in a dodgem car cut loose from the carnival.

Now, as the miles dropped away and Loudon was near, a realization occurred: I had been being ambushed by intense and strange fears for exactly as long as I had owned a motorcycle, since they had begun coming shortly after Tad left. The motorcycle and the fear had coexisted for over ten years, merging, separating only under threat of force, joining again in the dark of my mind, being driven apart once more by another type of reckoning. On a bike, I thought, I am hurtling toward what I imagine is a fearful future, but I am using a fearless means to do so. It's odd as hell.

But it's not, either. Riding *is* dangerous. Riding is dynamic. It is something to look forward to, and it is something to hesitate about—something of both at precisely the same time. It is something to work at, for me, something to surrender to. Close your eyes tonight, I think. You will dream of this ride.

# POSTSCRIPT

*I love to sail forbidden seas, and land on barbarous coasts.*
—*Melville*, Moby-Dick

When you ride, you travel light. As you would see, this is one of biking's great virtues. You take along what is in your stomach, and on your back, and whatever fits into the tankbag between the tools and the rain gear, all of which you will need sooner or later, especially the electrical tape.

At some point, you will throw your gloves to the ground in exasperation. Something's broke. But that is also the source of a strange relief: You've got to fix it. So you discover that you brought your wits along too, those rusty mechanisms that work on old-fashioned principles, wherein you can see the crankshaft turn and the chain progress and the up, down, up, down of levers and legs. For this brief time, you get to forget the maddening prevalence of electronic impulses you cannot feel and shiny boxes you cannot get inside of, and you become the scavenger the gods of old intended you to be. Sink your teeth into this one, the silent motorcycle says; go ahead, see if that bottle cap by your feet will be of use. Of course, it is a relief only in retrospect, after you've had a night or two in the bed that seems so far away now from the darkening roadside it could almost make you weep. Yes, the relief comes much later, and even then you may not know it is relief, because it has been applied directly to your soul. And later this whole sweaty, lonely frustration will be further transformed by the requirements of the campfire-story form into laughs and empathetic nods and you too will laugh as if it happened to someone else long ago, to a character out of a book.

When the sun is at the correct angle, your shadow races next to you as you fly along. The dark shape is your own hair streaming out, a mobile portrait in the medium of light on asphalt. It's a peculiar sight, but the start it gives is not like when you catch yourself in a mirror. This one is almost someone else, mysterious, featureless, perhaps even fearless.

When everything is going just fine, you can raise your weight off the saddle by standing on the pegs and the air itself seems to carry you; the smells of countryside or suburb or industrial fief are immediately upon you, then gone. There are uncanny presences all around. Rotting pumpkins, manure, road salt, Spanish moss in humid wind, a scent like a million burning tires in the yellow sky over Newark, pine, oyster shells. Some will never get a name. Not half of them would reach you in a car, even with all the windows down. This weekend, for four miles, I had the odor of cigarette in my nostrils, from the lit end hanging out from the pickup truck ahead. Then again, some smells just tell you you are riding much too close behind.

The temperature, too, and permeable quality of the air is astonishingly variable, as if you were riding in a slo-mo dream in and out of rooms as numerous and surprising as those at Versailles. As you're riding along in the warm envelope of a summer night, the country ether a pillow of moist hay and fecund dirt, suddenly there will be a blast of cold from a pocket held in the hollow of some land beyond you in the dark; you shiver, then you're out of it again, back in a caress of warmth. The coming rainstorm announces itself first in the quick change of the air, carrying you into the mounting thickness that only later comes out and shows itself.

Riding is something that hovers between you and the road. Or rather, it is about removing as much as possible between you and the road, about extending yourself past the very vehicle that enables you to feel the road in the first place. So in one sense it's about the way a road moves past you.

It is possible to feel more alone on a motorcycle than anywhere at rest. When you're sealed in your apartment, or even standing in a secret field halfway up a mountain, there is always the chance that someone could find you; someone could call, could spot you from a plane, could come walking up at any moment. Knowing where I can hide if necessary is always on my mind, and where else but on a bike is there somewhere truly safe to be? On a bike, there are people all around, in a car in the next lane not five feet away, but they can't get you. You may communicate with the friends who ride along by using signals, but you can't talk. You are spared the burden of words. There is so little privacy anywhere these days that this knowledge feels like the last available comfort, in the absence of knowing there is some-place left on earth not infected with Colonial brick houses or cut through by a new Wal-Mart's access road.

Your thoughts are pinned close to your head by the helmet, where they may exit only a fraction of an inch from your scalp but then stay to buzz around, thousands of little trapped sand flies.

At no time, though, are you more joyfully alone than when it is raining. Often it's lovely to sit indoors and hear the soft whiteness of rain hitting glass or roof; with the lights on, in your dry castle, you smugly note how close and yet how far the bad weather is. The safe protection of the walls seems to belong to you, a projection of your skin. On a bike, the house's walls shrink to become the rainsuit's thin rind. The water hits it, but you are cozy enough inside. The fact that you can feel it landing on you without touching you brings the impression of haven into high relief—which is pretty damn ironic, since there can be no greater danger than riding in the rain.

Sensing the tires slip a bit under you in a car is not usually cause for celebration, but you can generally regain control easily if you're a decent driver. Recovery is not so simple when there are only two wheels in question. Riding on the back of a friend's bike through southern Germany's excessive picturesqueness, I took in the passing sights secure in the knowledge that he was as able a rider as they make. We took the turns at a good lean, overcoming an instinctual fear to emerge into the pleasure of having done so. Then a light drizzle started washing the streets to a gleam, and everything changed. My seat noticed it first, a slight side-to-side motion that I almost thought was in my head. When we stopped, I asked if I had in fact felt something, and my friend just looked pale in response. So I mounted up behind another member of the party, whose experience was equal but whose rear tire was less bald. Confidence returned, even though the rain now fell in hard sheets. The beer at lunch I allowed myself as consolation for being a mere passenger was having its effect under the canopy of trees. The next thing I knew my hands thrust themselves into the air. Every sinew pulled itself tight. In a flash the seat had gone out from under me, shimmied curtly side to side to side. Then in a second it was over, and we were going on as before. Who knows? It could have been a bit of patched paving, slippery tar, some chameleon oil behind the sheen of wet.

But no matter how treacherous it is, I still love riding in the rain. It is so lulling, peaceful. Sound is slurred by the shh-shhing of the water, which rolls in little estuaries from the treads of the tires. Every other minute or so you reach up and wipe away the beading rain that blurs the vision through the shield, only to have it re-collect in seconds. Breath fogs the view from inside, and when you crack the shield open a bit to dispel the moisture, rain pelts your lips. Your hands feel strangely distant on the controls, because of the addition of thick rubber or Gore-Tex; you feel insulated or blown up, like Michelin's Bibendum. What's going on out there seems a million miles away, though it's on top of you, and driving at you, and kicked up behind you in that poetically arcing stream from the spinning wheel. The thoughts rise and collect as they always do, but now they're a dry ceiling. If you're doing this at night, perils and isolation both are intensified: the headlights of cars coming toward you refract and brighten to a glare on your face shield; the buffeting wind coming off the passing vehicles pushes you sideways for a moment, and all you can do is hang on. Perhaps that's the source of the comfort I feel—lack of alternatives. Life simplified at long last.

The small glow emanating from the lighted dials is a portable beacon that remains both ahead and calmly with you. The sight of the instrument panel's little light in the greater dark puts me in mind of a tiny spaceship floating on its way through a benighted universe of unfathomed spread. The headlight glances off the slick leaves at the edge of the road, and what is beyond that quick beam waits there for you to arrive upon it and briefly launch it into existence before consigning it back to what is behind in the black.

With the dampened sound, thoughts become louder. The only thing beside yourself that you can hear, somewhere beneath you, is a steady throb of engine. It is all there is to keep you anchored to the world. All the rest, all the earth, is rain.

This is so untroubled a state of affairs that sometimes catatonia wants to overtake me—in spite of all the ways I try to remind myself about the dangers of believing what it is convenient to believe. I recall riding up the New Jersey Turnpike in a dead rain near midnight on a Sunday, the traffic as unceasing as the storm. I had been doing sixty in the same lane for what seemed like forever, which is what the turnpike is all about. Then I needed to change. I did it as I had dozens of times before on this same road, when it was dry. This time, crossing the lane divider and those handy little reflectors put there for the safety of cars, my rear wheel met the plastic and for a second spun. It was in that class of events that are simple and quick, so immediate they seem to precede their own occurrence, as when your foot slips in a dream and thus makes a cliff appear. I woke up to a moment of blinding panic, then it was over. For a mile or two my heart was near my gullet, and I thought about all the possibilities that could have been realized. I'd like to say that for the rest of the ride I was more careful, and I probably was to the degree that anyone can manage life's risks, but I still couldn't begin the accounting of everything that hadn't occurred to me yet, a voodoo list that I believed once mastered would deliver me from evil. There is so much that must remain incalculable, a fact better accepted than kicked against. It is a hoary lesson repeated, if I would listen, in every revolution of the wheels.

Does all this sound like a rhapsody? I both mean it to and don't. There are two bikes in the world that belong to me. One is the real one, which sits in the garage on Union Street with a rear-drive leak and clapped-out front suspension begging for new springs. This is the one I've done about 35,000 miles on, a white Moto Guzzi Lario, two cylinders with four valves per head, small and lean with sixteen-inch wheels front and back, Italian-red rims. I've spent what must amount to a couple of seven-day weeks in the rain on it. This is the bike I have finally finished payments on, have been up to Canada and down to the Gulf Coast on, wish for the Al-Can highway on. The other is the perfect vehicle, the bike of the mind. This is the motorcycle that is lavish in its gifts and lessons. Sometimes I fear it; often I dream about it; sometimes I love it with longing as if it were already gone.

Here, now, on the cusp of winter, I walk the sidewalks of Brooklyn and descend into the subway to wait. Down there, all of a sudden, I walk into an ambush of memory: a peculiar dead end somewhere, in a coal town in Pennsylvania at dusk a couple of years ago when, following the route signs to a more familiar road, I found myself heading into a cul-de-sac near a deserted town park and a cemetery up the hill beyond. The road ended smack at the burying ground's driveway. I turned about and did the circuit again, just to make certain I hadn't misread the signs, which I obviously had, but right now there seems something more imperative about that dead end. I never thought about it until this moment, at the Seventh Avenue station, and now my mind is filled with it. The purple light at the edge of the fall sky, the dark trees rising up, the road disappearing among the graves.

Or it comes to me, another time, that I'm in Tennessee at night.

It's so black I don't know what's on either side of the road, behind the shallow vault of trees and pavement illuminated by my headlight. The road seems to tilt downward into the cold and dark green, although I know it's flat. Up ahead is the cauldron from which they sell the boiled peanuts, its bright steam, then more blackness beyond. It feels, in my recollection, as if nothing preceded this particular moment. But I can surely feel the cold right through my clothes, view the scene coming toward me.

Sometimes I get a couple of those weirdly floating moments in a day, as I'm going about my business. Then I'm quickly cut loose and adrift in this sea of arbitrary memory. The thing is, the only thoughts that come to me like this are memories of riding. Nothing else survives the precise weight of those sensations. Each moment of those 35,000 miles seems to be catalogued in some deep archive, and occasionally the wind flips up one of the index cards they're each on and it's suddenly there, bobbing at the surface of consciousness, along with a ghost perception of the temperature and smell of the air. This is the perfume of the past. Future scents wait by the road.

ACKNOWLEDGMENTS

Over the years that I have been riding motorcycles, and the years of that time when I was working on this book, I have been helped by various people in various ways. Some of them will have to remain nameless but not unthanked, such as the fellows in Europe who picked up their phones one evening, and though they had never met the stranded American on the other end of the line, spent much time patiently attempting to diagnose a breakdown problem from a distance of hundreds of miles.

Those whose names I do know, and have given me much kind help, are Franz Nachod, Armen Amirian, Luc Van Vossel, David Smith, and Ivar de Gier. Thank you so much. Others who have assisted with my endeavors, biking, writing, or both, and who deserve recognition are John Wittner, Robert Fulton, Hilton Webb, Jr., Bob Nevola, Bud Greenberg, Frank Wedge of the MGNOC, Kees Visser, Scott Emmons, Erica Smith, Peter Dervis, Julie Kramer, Bob Sweeny, and Ron Hand. Special thanks are due to my parents-in-law, Denise and Lucien Sante, whose garage has become my bike's comfortable domicile, and who always welcome me into their home, whether I am on a periodic mechanical mission or not. Photographers and friends extraordinaire Chris Felver and Erica Lansner also have my deep gratitude.

John Leffler really deserves a category unto himself. In addition to his unbounded generosity as a friend and accessible technical resource, he has read the manuscript of this book and saved me from public exposure of many gaffes. The mistakes that remain are examples of my persistence.

Brooke Alderson and Peter Schjeldahl seem genetically incapable of being anything but unflaggingly kind; I have been the beneficiary of this predisposition too many times to count. But I am especially thankful to Peter for his gift of the perfect subtitle, another proof that he is, in the most inclusive sense, a poet first and last.

I am enormously indebted to Colin Harrison of *Harper's* magazine, which originally published part of this work. This book would not be a book (for it would not have come to the notice of a publisher) without his interest and hard work, and the support of Lewis Lapham. Their openness, intelligence, and humaneness make them truly rare among editors. I must also thank Wendy Lesser of *The Threepenny Review* for earlier publishing another bit and thereby heartening a disheartened writer.

My publisher, W. W. Norton, has in Amy Cherry a very fine editor. Her enthusiasm and sensitivity provided the proper growing medium for this book, and her fine-tuning improved it greatly. I really appreciate her encouragement and efforts.

I gratefully acknowledge the cheerful help of the staff of the Prints and Photographs division of the Library of Congress.

To my parents, of course, go the ultimate thanks. I respect their wit, style, and talents so greatly I have often prayed that some ghost vestige of what makes them so extraordinary might become visible in these pages.

The friendship of Polly Hanson has buoyed me throughout the process of writing, and well beyond. I am lucky to have her in my life.

I cannot thank Bob Alvarez, Arlette Mann, Liz Smith and especially Linda Krause half enough. They have individually and collectively enriched my life, and in part my ability to complete this book is due to them and the work we do together.

My husband, Luc Sante, has gone on this journey with me, in spirit if not on two wheels. When I grew frustrated with my inability to read the map, he gently took it and turned it right side up. He encouraged me to go farther. And he was the home to which I returned so eagerly. This book, and everything else, is for him.